THE COURAGE TO BE BLIND

Juanita Vedder

Quantum Discovery

A LITERARY AGENCY

Library of Congress Control
Number: 2025904223

ISBN
978-1-963254-25-9 (Paperback)
978-1-963254-26-6 (eBook)

TABLE OF CONTENTS

PREFACE

It is my honor to say that I have written another book called *In the Midst of Pain* under the name Juanita R. McNeil. I am greatly honored to say that I have been happily married since I wrote my first book. My husband, Frank Vedder, has been so wonderful to me and very supportive in helping me with both of my books. He has been with me through all the trials and pain I had to endure while I have been trying to live a positive and productive life. Though my journey has not been easy, my husband has endured a lot of my pain. And my children have endured so much too. I do not know how I could have lived such a blessed life if it were not for God and my family helping me to pull through it one day at a time. To me, living with blindness is a beautiful stepping stone toward a better and brighter future. Just when I think life cannot get any worse, it got better. And that, my friend, is all the work of God. I give God all the glory due Him, for I really do believe that the words of this book are inspired by Him. I could not have done this on my own. Thank you, Jesus, for all your blessed word.

INTRODUCTION

To all who read this book, it is my desire for you to be inspired by these writings. I have based this book upon true and inspiring events of myself and other people who are suffering from blindness. Due to the painful tragedies that my blindness has caused me, it has been my goal to write this book in hopes of reaching out to others who are having the same difficult time living their life blind and dealing with the effects of their blindness. I would like to introduce this book to you about the courageous faith it takes for a blind person to live in a dark world with no light to lead them.

My blindness has inspired me to push life beyond its limits and to reach for its full potential. My blindness became my stepping stone to living my life in the world of reality. It was then reality became real for me. Due to lack of faith and the lack of courage to persevere, the reality of blindness has taken the lives of those who could not walk by faith. You see, blindness is like having cancer; it eats away at your vision to see the world, and it steals your reason to live. When you walk by sight and your sight fails you, then all you have left is faith. But when your faith fails you, then all you have left is a hopeless life that death seeks out. A blind person is not able to look into their future and visualize their dreams. Blindness can destroy more than just a person's vision. It can destroy their life. My blindness has taught me to stay very close to God, to trust in Him completely and to always walk by faith and not by sight, for I know that God will lead me through the valley of death and that He will bring the good out of the evil that comes against me. I know that God will do the same for you. Your blindness is not the end of your life, for it is only the beginning of your journey.

Though my eyes have failed me, God has given me His eyes to see. And now I see my blindness as a blessing in disguise. God has brought me to a whole new level in life. The more I walk by faith, the more I overcome my obstacles. It is too often that some people who are blind give up hope of living life to the fullest and seeking to find a better future for themselves. For it seems like when you start losing your vision, you then start losing your will to live.

The pressures of life and trying to keep up with today's society can be very overbearing and to demanding for a blind person. Blindness can hold you back and make life more difficult to endure. Life's challenges are difficult enough, but being blind only makes it worse. I struggle every day just living with the challenges that life seems to create for me. My life is a challenging journey, and it seems to be an all uphill battle for me. But at least I do know that victory is waiting for me at the top, and I will succeed!

My blindness is a gift from God and not just some bad eye problem. It is a gift that I can benefit from! For it is only through God that I see my blindness as a gift and not a burden. May God bless you as you read this book! I hope you find this book useful and inspiring.

My Greatest Challenges

Challenges! Life is so full of them, and they come upon us unexpectedly! Just living life in general is a devastating challenge for me! Challenges will bring a lot of pain in some type of form. Whether it is physically, emotionally, mentally, or even spiritually, pain is pain. The pain that challenges give, will either make you stronger, or it will break you down. Unfortunately, for some of my friends, their greatest challenge of being blind has pushed them to their graves. Even I have been nearly pushed to an early grave, except that God said no to it. The more I try to give up in life, the more God pushes me further into my future of living beyond my limits. God has given me the strength each time I am faced with the challenges of being blind. I do hope that God will do the same for you (Psalm 29:11)!

I have never experienced any types of challenges that did not bring some form of pain. If there is no pain to feel, then there is no challenge ever too great. The greater the challenge, the greater the pain! This is why it takes courage to be blind. It takes courage to step up to reality and face each challenging day whether you are blind or not, but more so for a blind person! It takes more courage for the blind to face what they cannot see! But, to me, it is the fear of the unknown that brings such a challenge to my world. But my challenges also bring me blessing in disguise. Living in darkness is not a pretty sight to see. It's very scary. It is a place where I am alone and no one can help me but God Himself. Being blind puts me in my own world that no one else understands unless they are living in my world with me. Not even my family can live in my world and understand what I am going through. I have even found it difficult for a blind person to understand what another blind person is going through. I will explain that later about me and my friends who are blind. Just remember, the less your challenges are, the weaker you become, and eventually you give up striving for a better life to live, and soon you give up in life. But why do we give up?

We give up because it just gets too hard to keep on striving for what we cannot see! It is hard to fight for a future that is too dark and lonely, and sometimes it just feels like there is nothing left to hope for. It becomes too hard to see a reason to move on! Another person can tell you that they are blind too, but how do I know if they really are blind or not if I cannot see them to know. How does a blind person really know the truth except just to believe!

There is no reason to feel pain and suffer the consequences of it if there is no challenge that will make you change for the better or for the worse. People will just stay in their comfort zones. I find that there is no life living in a comfort zone. And if challenges were made easy, then there would be no such thing as faith! I do believe that God creates trials that will challenge us so that we can put our hope, trust, and faith in Him. For what reason would we have hope and faith if there was no challenging trials in our lives? Everything happens for a reason. There would be no reasons for pain and no reasons to suffer! So, what is the point of life if we are not challenged? Life in itself is a challenge to live! Challenges are what I live for! My character is formed by my challenges. Challenges are my greatest tests in life, and they are such a blessing to have. Challenges are what bring out the best in me, and they show me who I really am!

What does challenge mean? How would one describe it? How would you describe it? As for me, I describe it as a test or something that would cause me hardship in achieving my goals. Challenges are the driving force that moves me beyond myself Life's most challenging moments are what helps me to push life beyond its limits! There is no such thing as living life unless you are challenged to push it further!

For me, my greatest challenge has been my blindness due to the fact that I live in both worlds. I have very little tunnel vision left, and my right eye only has half of that. I have no night vision, and I have no peripheral vision or depth perception. And also, in what vision I do have left, there are blind spots. Since my vision is poor, I am constantly falling down, tripping over things, or running into things. Walking across the street is a challenge in itself because I do not always see the cars when I am walking in the crosswalk, and, yes, I have almost gotten hit a few times. Now that's scary. But the most difficult and most fearful challenge I ever have is life itself. I cannot and will not escape life or the challenges that life gives me. Believe me, if there was a way, I would probably try.

Now, when it comes time for me to just go places with my kids and just try and enjoy the day, I get hurt. There is this one day that I was with my daughter at the mall, and I wanted to go into this vitamin store, and so we did. I asked the lady at the register about a certain vitamin, and there was a gentleman behind me who said, "Follow me, I will help you! "As I turned around to follow him, I tripped over their display and fell hard.

The gentleman and my daughter asked me if I was okay. I said no. I was hurting really bad, and my arm was bleeding. But I was so embarrassed that all I wanted to do was get out of the store. So my daughter helped me up, and I left. I finally got my arm to quit bleeding. It was a bad scratch. But the problem was I had torn my ligament from my middle finger, and the ligament was way up in the upper part of my hand. A few weeks later, I had surgery done on my hand, but I still have problems with my middle finger. All this was because I could not see what was below me when I had turned around to follow the gentleman. This happened only a few years ago.

I also have four pinched nerves in my neck from hitting my forehead. One day I was at McDonald's with my daughter and my grandson. My grandson fell down, and I went to see if he was okay when I ran into one of the bars. I hit my forehead so hard that I thought I broke my neck. My neck was severely sore for the longest time, and I had to go to the hospital later. The doctor put me on pain medicine and something for tight muscles, all because I cannot see anything above me when I am looking straight ahead. Other frightening times are when I fall in the street, and a car would come around the corner. This has happened a few times, and I have never been so scared in my life. There are many other accidents, but I'm sure you get the picture.

I guess the greatest challenge of being blind is just trying to live a decent life and enjoy God's beauty of it. But life becomes such a challenge for me because when I get hurt so much, it is hard to live a happy life. So the challenge is for me to persevere and endure the pain while feeling happy and blessed. Now that is what I call a challenge—to be happy when you're feeling pain! Praise God for that! The only way I have met this challenge head-on and overcome it is with the grace of God helping me. For He has given me His strength to carry on! God blesses me when I get hurt!

Now the sad thing is people think that I am not blind because I do not look blind and I do not act blind. If I bump into someone at the store, they think I am drunk or on drugs, and people get very rude with me. But when I use my cane, people are very polite to me, and they go out of their way to help me. It's hard for me to accept blindness because I feel odd when I use my cane. It takes courage just to face the day not knowing what will happen and not knowing if I will become totally blind when I wake up or when I am out and about somewhere without my family.

For a blind person, it becomes even more of a challenge when people judge you by your looks or your actions. So, what does a blind person look like, and how do we act around other people? Some people think that we are normal while others think we are different. We get treated the way that people think they should treat us, whether it is bad or good. Some people even go as far as being rude and disrespectful or think that we are weird. It is hard living in this world being blind. We just don't fit in. Sometimes I feel like an alien because I don't fit in this same world as visual people do. Do I adapt to people, or do they adapt to me? No matter what, it just feels weird. Just trying to live an ordinary life seems to get in the way. Now that's depressing itself!

I'm not sure what I would do if I lose all my vision! It's hard enough just trying to live as I am now! I don't know if it would be easier or harder. I do know that I will never be prepared to lose all my vision. To me, that would be the greatest challenge of all! So what is your greatest challenge? We all have them!

In February of 2012, I went to school for my blindness. There, I had a lot of challenging circumstances! One of the hardest challenges was learning to accept my blindness and know how to deal with it. During my activities of learning, I had to be totally blindfolded so that I would know how to live in this world totally blind. It is totally different for me because I just have the hardest time trying to accept going blind, that someday I will lose all my vision. No matter how much schooling I have had, I will still never be prepared to lose the rest of my vision. During my time in school, I did everything that I needed for basic living with no vision. I cooked and cut up vegetables, I learned Braille, and that is a whole new language of its own. Reading with your finger is a challenge because all the dots feel the same. But I did it.

Walking outside was the most fearful part for me due to the fact I have fallen in the streets so many times. I had to really pay attention to my hearing and to what direction the cars were going. Learning how to cross a very busy street with no audio crosswalk was the greatest challenge. Knowing *when* to cross became very difficult and confusing. The hard part was trying to listen to the traffic when it is very busy. There are so many people talking, walking, dogs barking, and cars driving in and out of parking lots. Not knowing when to cross is very scary for being totally blindfolded. It took me nine months of schooling before I was able to cross the street, and even then it is still very hard to do. Living in this world blind is almost impossible, but it can be done because blind people do not have a choice. For we just cannot take off our blindfolds and look where we are going. No, we have to rely on our other senses. Hearing and paying very close attention are the most important. I do not know how a deaf and blind person can even make it through this hard journey known as life!

Paying attention to your surroundings is the most difficult thing to do when other people, especially other drivers, do not pay attention to you. Car wrecks happen all the time. Even people who have vision to see all around them get hit in crosswalks. Now do you know how scary it is for a blind person to walk around in this world where people do not pay any attention? It is hard enough for me to be in my own home and running into the walls all the time. It is a challenge just to get out of bed in the middle of the night just to use the bathroom across the hall. Can you imagine what it is like being outside?

I did an experiment with my grown children and their father. I had a pair of painted black glasses, and I asked them to put on the glasses and walk around outside. They did for a few seconds, and then they took them off and said, "No way." Then I asked my daughter to cut up some onions and celery, and she did a little bit and said, "No, I can't do this! It's too hard!" Now they know what I am going through, and even then, they cannot grasp the feeling. They just cannot imagine being blind.

Too many people take advantage of the gift of eyesight that God gives them. There's that old saying that goes, "You do not realize what you have until you lose it!" That, my friend, is so true! So never forget that! I praise God that I have not lost all my vision. I believe He is keeping me from going totally blind for a reason that I do not know yet. God is the only one I need for this journey. No one else will do!

Now I have noticed that life becomes even more depressing when I allow my blindness to become a burden instead of a blessing. God wants me to use my blindness as a stepping stone. I know that God will teach me how to use my blindness as a stepping stone! I experienced a lot of this depression when I was in school for the blind. It is easy to allow yourself to get depressed and give up hope on living a better future for yourself. I was there when some of them have lost their will to live because they did not know how to accept and deal with their blindness. Like I said, it's easy to do, for I have experienced it for myself. But the more I lean on God, the more He helps me to understand that no matter how blind I am, my life is just beginning. I believe that God is using me as an inspiration to others in encouraging them not to give up in life. We may have lost our vision, but we have not lost our life! It may seem like it, considering people think that vision is your life; we think that without vision, we have no life to live for. But I believe that God has special plans for us blind people.

When I was in school, I have tried to explain to other students about how to use their blindness as a stepping stone because I believe that our blindness is a blessing in disguise instead of a heavy burden weighing us down in life. This is what makes the journey seem so impossible. The weight of our burden drags us down so much that the journey becomes too painful to endure, so we give up too soon instead of persevering through the pain that we all too often have to endure. But I know we do not have to endure our pain on our own because God is with us. God will lighten our load if we give it to Him.

The saddest part is when you lose your will to live and desire to strive for a better future, and then you lose the will to envision your blindness as a blessing instead of a burden. As a blind person, I have asked what the point of life is if I cannot see the beauty of God's precious life. This is why I walk by faith and not so much by sight (2 Corinthians 5:7). I have to depend on God for direction in life, and I need Him to lead me, for I know that I cannot walk this journey by myself. Even people with vision use their vision as a way of life just to live and get around. They use their vision as if their life depends on it. But vision is not your life. It is only a part of your body that helps you obtain your basic needs. A blind person can still live life to the fullest. It is all in the attitude toward life. God has certainly changed my attitude about life. My blindness is now my stepping stone, and I have now stepped up in life. Thank you, God! So, think about vision for a moment! Our entire outlook on life is seen through our vision. So, without our vision, how can we see our future? A person may lose their vision, but their life still remains! That is until you sink into such a deep depressed state of mind, then eventually it will take your life to your grave!

There are so many people who just do not acknowledge the point in living without their eyesight. It is God's grace that keeps me holding on. It is sad too because some people even allow death to come upon them instead of striving for a better way to endure their pain. It's easier to take the easy way out instead of enduring pain. Believe me, I have tried. Pain is what makes us grow, and pain is what gives us a sense of purpose in life. But many people do not think of it this way! Many blind people become too overwhelmed to push life beyond its limits; it is just too hard to persevere. So, they give up too easily and too soon! Think about what it would be like for you if you were blind. How would you react to life's pain and struggles?

I have one brother who has the same eye disease as I have, except he is completely blind now. He has pretty much given up on life, and he has tried to commit suicide twice that I know of.

He is too weak to endure his pain and suffering. I have tried to commit suicide too, but self-inflicted death is not the answer! It will only make matters worse for those loved ones who are left behind to deal with the loss of your presence.

When I think about the time I tried to end my life, I think about how selfish I was. Now I thank God that I did not succeed in death. Now I think about how blessed that I am for what vision I do have left. Though I struggle and fight against this eye disease, I still feel blessed, for I know that God is with me and that He still has a plan for my life. This is the promise that I hang on to from God, and this is what keeps me going! The difference between me and my brother is that I rely on God for the things in life that I need. This is how I endure my perseverance! God has given me the courage I need to walk this journey through the shadow of the valley of death.

When I was in blind school, I noticed that persevering through the challenges of life and enduring the pain that it gives is just too challenging for some blind people to endure. I have encountered some people with anger caused by their blindness, and I do understand why. Life gets very frustrating when you cannot see what you are doing. I have found myself frustrated a many times too. Vision is a very precious gift from God, and it is not intended to be abused or taken for granted, though people do anyways.

The beauty of having vision is to see the beauty of life. People are too busy living life in the fast lane to slow down long enough to acknowledge God's beauty. One thing is for sure about being blind, I have nothing but time to slow down and enjoy God's presence filling the air around me. I still have my hearing to hear the birds sing, and I still have my sense of smell to take in the scent of fresh flowers blooming. And those I will not take for granted. Instead, I take time to thank God for His beauty and for allowing me to wake each morning to breathe the precious air that He has given us so that I can enjoy His beauty that is all around me.

Too often, people with vision do not see what is important in life because they are too busy looking for other things that seem more important. And of course, people with vision will walk by sight and not their faith. O you of little faith, as God says it. The good thing about being blind is that I am in no big hurry to get to somewhere that I may not reach. People are always too busy being in such a hurry to get where they are going, and yet they miss their destination—or shall I say, they missed the mark! They are too busy going somewhere, and yet they are getting nowhere.

Just remember, you don't realize what you have until you lose it, and then it is too late to get it back so you can appreciate it. People need to realize what they have now and appreciate it because what the good Lord gives, the good Lord can also take. It's odd how people can wander around in this world and live their life aimlessly with no goals or dreams. As a blind person, I do have goals and dreams. I will not take life for granted. I will stop and acknowledge the beauty of God's grace, and I will thank Him for it! How about you?

They say that life is what you make it! But if that were true, then why do blind people have such a hard time trying to make life better for themselves? All we can do is just try and live life to the fullest the best that we can! At least that is what I am doing! For I did not choose to be blind, but blindness has chosen me! Though I try to make the best of life for the good, it is still not as good as when I once had more vision! Except now I have learned to respect and appreciate life and the blessings that God bestows upon me more. I praise God for all that I am! When I did have vision, life was easier, and I was able to do more things and enjoy more of life's little things. As they say, it's the little things that count. I seriously believe that! My blindness has become a disability for me. What I once have been able to do, I no longer can now. My blindness has kept me from doing the things that I enjoyed in life, like driving. I am no longer able to drive and be independent. I'm not able to walk as well as I used to without getting hurt. I cannot ride a bicycle anymore or play on go-karts with my kids. There are many fun things in life I am no longer able to do, and that is very depressing for me. I cannot even walk on a sidewalk without getting hurt because of the uneven cracks. Just as of today, I was walking on the sidewalk, and I walked right into a metal light pole and bloodied my nose. I was then rushed to the hospital, where I found out that my nose is broken, and all I was doing was just walking. My blind stick somehow missed the pole! I applied for a guide dog a few months ago, but I was told that I walk too well for a guide dog, yet I am always getting hurt. My blindness has caused me to lose a lot of my independence, and now I have to depend on my family or Dial-a-Ride to get around. My blindness has gotten in my way of even the simplest things that a toddler can do! To me, mentally that is painful.

My blindness has even thrown my balance off, so now I fall easier. Try to walk with your eyes closed and see how much balance you have. Vision does play a big role in a person's balance. Even with a guide dog, I still need to know when to cross a street and what direction I am going in because the dog does not know that. The guide dog just keeps you from running into things or lets you know if there is a car in your way or any other objects that can hurt you. A dog is color blind, so they do not know what color the streetlight is. This is why it is so important for a blind person to rely on their hearing and the other senses. That is what I did learn in blind school.

Now, in today's society, it is even harder to cross a street with lights because of those newer cars called hybrid. They are so quiet, and that is what makes it so hard to hear if they are moving or stopped. So, then I rely on my other senses. This is called a sense of direction. Here is how your sense of direction feels like. Blindfold yourself and put your hand over your ear, but do not touch your ear. Wave your hand back and forth without touching your ear. Stop your hand when you sense it close to your ear. This is what sense of direction feels like. Though you cannot feel what is there or see what is there, you know that something is there. This is what it is like when a blind person tries to cross a street when a hybrid car is there. In some towns, there are no audio streetlights, so I have to go by my hearing or my sense of direction.

Here is what so hard for me. No matter how careful I am, I still come close to getting hit by a car because the driver either did not see me, or they are just not paying any attention. No matter what, being blind is just hard to live with. And it is so scary just to walk outside, not knowing what will happen next. After running into that metal light pole, I am now scared just to walk anywhere. I just feel like giving up, but I know I can't. I struggle so hard just to survive this journey that will never end. I hate being blind, but there is nothing I can do about it. Every day becomes more and more of a challenge for me. When you come to that point in your life where you are losing your sense of natural human instincts, then you become paralyzed by your own fear, which sets in and tells you that you can no longer do anything. This type of fear will bring death to you sooner than it should have. Death comes too easily and quicker than expected! This type of fear will cause anyone to lose their will to survive the hard-core challenges that life itself will bring you.

Disabilities come in different ways for many different reasons. And it does not matter what type of disability you have. They are all challenging, especially when life itself is a challenge of its own. Learning how to accept it and deal with it and still be able to give God all the glory for it is the biggest challenge one can face. I not only struggle with my blindness, I struggle with depression too. I try to keep a positive attitude while trying to inspire others to keep on moving forward in life and be happy. But it seems like the more I get hurt, the more I get depressed. It seems like I cannot win for losing. Am I really getting anywhere in life, or am I just living to be living? So have you ever thought this about your life? Believe me, it is easy to do!

Now here is another challenge that I struggle with every day. I was just recently diagnosed with ADHD. It is some type of attention disorder, and apparently, I had it all my life. But when I was a child, it was called hyperactive disorder, and I was medicated for that. Then I was also diagnosed with restless leg syndrome. This is a very big struggle for me with my blindness because my legs go faster than my eyes can see where I am going or what I am doing, and therefore, my brain cannot respond quickly enough, so I get hurt. This is why I struggle with keeping a positive attitude. But I have God in my life, and He is the only one that gives me His grace and strength to keep on living. Thank you, Lord.

The more I get hurt, the lesser human value I feel, I start feeling like a child who constantly needs to be watched over and cared for. I can't stand it. And then my depression sets in more. I am taking sixty milligrams of Prozac just to stay halfway sane. That's enough to make a horse laugh! Except I am not laughing. This medicine does not make me laugh. It only helps keep me from going insane. Another reason for me to feel less of a human is because I am losing a big part of my body, and without my eyesight, I cannot function very well. God says that I must keep on striving for the best in what life has to offer me. God also says that my life is not over just because my eyes have failed me. I know that God has a plan for my life, so I must stick to His plan. I know that God is the reason why I am still alive to tell my story and to be an inspiration to others who needs an encouraging word for the day. God has given unto me the gift of inspiration that I must respect.

Have you ever noticed that no matter what your disability is, and no matter what your challenges are, pain will always be a part of the problem that you are constantly dealing with? No matter what you do in life or how you live your life, there is just no escaping your pain. What about reality? Is reality painful too? I believe that reality and pain go hand in hand, for you cannot experience one without the other. That is what I believe. Reality causes pain because pain is real. What do you think? Now, as for me, facing reality is the most difficult challenge that I face because reality is an everyday issue with me. The reality of being blind is the challenge I face every day.

Now for the longest time, I could not or, shall I say, would not accept the reality of being blind. I am still trying to learn how to accept reality, and at times I feel like I never will accept it. It just becomes too painful to endure. People say that I need to accept my blindness for what it is because there is nothing that will ever change that. Well, that may well be true, but would you accept it if you were the one who is blind? Yes, of course life is never easy! It's never easy for anyone! Life just brings on more challenges! I believe that is how and why we grow. Well, that is what I have experienced in my lifetime. To me, life becomes more painful the harder and greater the challenges are, and to endure the reality of my pain becomes a greater challenge for me to accept. Now try to persevere through that!

I have studied the word *challenge*, and it amazes me to know that the word in itself is challenging. The word *challenge* seems to be more of a challenge then the actual meaning of the word. The standard college dictionary explains it as to claim as due, to demand a contest with an invitation, or to dare to participate in. You see, to me, challenges are like taking a test! You are being tested to see if you can accomplish whatever it is that is challenging you. Challenges for a blind person seem almost impossible to take on because it means giving up on your dreams.

Now here is a sad but true story! I know a dear friend of mine who is doing this. She literally hates anything that is a challenge. When she was in school with me, she would constantly tell me that she hates school. "It is too hard for me," she would say! Then she would say, "I hate homework! I hate anything that makes me think or work my brain." She would rather have people to do things for her. It's easier if someone else does it for her. This is what I had to deal with when I was in school for my blindness. She literally hated to learn anything. She felt like it was no use because she was too blind and too old to learn anything new! Yes, that makes a lot of sense, but that is not the way to live. It wore me out because I was the one who took care of her until it got too hard on me. Then I had to stop taking care of her. She became a challenge for me.

Life is challenging enough having to take care of myself without having to take care of another blind person too. But I did try. When I stopped taking care of her and stopped feeling sorry for her, I then just helped her. I showed her what to do and how to do it. She then started to do things on her own! She did graduate and accomplish her certificate, and I am so proud of her. She is now able to do things for herself! And though she was angry with me while we were in school, we are now good friends. And now she lives on her own, and I go over there sometimes and help her, or I invite her out for dinner. She will always be a part of my life, and I still do things with her.

Losing your eyesight will make a person feel down and negative on life. A lot of the blind people that I went to school with felt like this. I have been around many blind people with a negative attitude toward life, and I used to be one of them. Being in school has really helped me with my attitude on life. But it is God who I praise the most! It is so sad to see people turn away from a challenge that can change their world for the better. This even happens to people with vision. How long does a person live like this before death claims their soul? I know two friends of mine that I went to school with who have passed away for the same reasons. The saddest part about this is that there is nothing anyone can do for them except to pray for them, and even then it is their choice to live or die. I went through this with my own brother.

I do often wonder why people do this to themselves! Lack of desire possibly! I even wonder at times why I do such things! Is it natural for human will to be like this? Well, I guess it will really make you stop and think! I think it is because we do not want to feel any more pain that is brought upon us through the things that challenges us. Pain becomes too painful to endure. But how often do we think about the reason why we feel so much pain and why we are being challenged? Not too often do people think of their pain as a challenge. They think of ways to just make it go away or wonder why they are in so much pain. Pain is the key factor that plays a major role in your life. For what kind of life would we live if we did not feel some type of pain? Just remember that pain brings change!

One thing I have come to realize is that pain will let you know that life is real, and it is the reason we are here on earth. And now that I have come to this knowledge, my relationship with God has really grown so much on a deeper level of understanding. And now I live for challenges, and I seek out the purposes for them. Greater things are yet to come! When God challenges me to do something, His challenges give my life more meaning and a better sense of direction and purpose. So, I have learned to take the pain from the challenges that are brought upon me and use them as an opportunity to grow and to love this life that God has given to me to live. Amen to that. Challenges will give you things to live for, and so now I am living a better life through the challenges that were bestowed upon my life.

Have you ever thought of challenges as a way of healing the human soul? I have, and it seems like it has healed my soul. Challenges give me more of an understanding that something big and great is about to happen in my life, and it will be for the good! I believe that challenges are a part of God's plan for our life. How else would you explain it? Challenging pain will bring you closer to God, and so therefore, God has healed my soul through the challenges that He has bestowed upon me! Though it may be painful, I know that I am with God and that He will see me through.

Here is another way of acknowledging challenges. The challenges we face today will affect our tomorrow and our future. Losing my vision made my brain automatically heighten my other senses! It's like I know where I am going even if I have never been there. I envision where I am going! So as long as you have a sense of direction and a purpose for living, then let your challenges become your opportunities to experience God's blessings upon your life. Please just enjoy the beauty of each given day when challenges bring you pain because there is a blessing in disguise of the beauty of God's painful challenges. You have one life to live, so do not cheat yourself out of the life that God has given you to live. God wants you to live for Him!

When you cheat yourself out of life, then life becomes of no value to you, and then it feels like life is not worth living for. I had a roommate who was like that. She just could not understand how her life could be of any value to her or anyone else. Since she lost her vision, she had felt like she had lost everything that was important in life. I worry about her and how long will she continue to live like this! She lost her vision through diabetes, and it is difficult for her to give herself shots. She was so angry all the time while we were in school, and she just hates life. I know it is easy to sink into this type of depressed state of mind because I have done it too. Now I have tried to help her, but she just lived the way she wanted to live and did not want my help. It is so sad to see people live like this, and yet there's not a thing you can do about it. A few months after I graduated from the blind school, I found out that she had passed away. It hurts just to think about this and why she lived the way she did! It is hard enough to be blind, but when you are sick too and have a very difficult time trying to take care of yourself, being blind just makes life harder to move forward, especially when you don't have a positive attitude.

My heart grieves for her soul because I am not sure how her relationship with God was. When I did talk to her about God and about how much that He loves her, she just started crying and was wondering if God really did love her. Her blindness gave her doubts about God! Her fate has been sealed through her death, and I know she cannot ask for forgiveness or come back to life and live her life differently. But as for me, I can learn from her mistakes. I can choose to live my life better and give God appreciation every day for keeping me alive and a blessing to others.

This goes for everyone who is living today, for we all can choose to live a better life. It is just a matter of having the will to do it! The choices that I have made today have given me a better hope for tomorrow and for my future! Whether it be good or bad, you will reap what you sow. In other words, you will get out of life what you put into it. So, make the right choices today and see a better tomorrow for yourself Just live for God!

Every day I am making changes that will benefit my future, and I make changes to be in the right standing with God. All this deals with making the choice. My faith in God keeps my dreams alive, with a special purpose to love people the way that God loves us! I look forward for the challenges that life brings me, and I am ready to tackle the pain it gives head-on. I am ready to move forward in life and be an inspiration for people so that they may have hope in God. I have promised myself that I will live my life to the fullest and push life beyond its limits with my faith in God. I know that God is with me because He promised that He would never leave me nor forsake me, and I know for sure that He would never forget about me.

2

Stepping Out of My Comfort Zone

When you leave God's house, you are stepping out of your comfort zone. I did not realize this until I moved to Seattle, Washington! I moved to Seattle February 19, 2012. I started school for my blindness on Monday, February 21, 2012.

As I attended the first week of school, everything was so different. My first week was evaluation. But my second week was the actual time of school. At this time in my life, I did not realize just how much my life was about to change. This is the challenge of a twist of faith. I did not know that God was planning on putting my faith to the test. But He did!

During the time that I remained in school, I may have made a lot of enemies. None of my classmates liked it when I would talk about God. Obviously, no one had a relationship with God, at least not the way that I did. Time went on. It seemed like the more enemies I attracted, the more my faith would grow. That is one of the best things that I did like about attracting enemies.

Well anyways, as the story goes, each day I went to school, it just got harder and harder. Each term, we got more and more new students while some graduated. Now for me the hardest part was in the beginning. Trying to accept my eye problem was to much for me, and knowing that no one liked for me to talk about God just made it that much harder for me to endure all this mental pain that I did not know how to deal with.

Now here is what is so weird. I knew that I was going blind and hade an eye problem. I also knew that I needed schooling to be able to learn how to live all over again. And I also knew that when I started school, I would be going to school with other blind students and some teachers. But what I did not know was that some of these blind people acted like they were babies and needed someone to take care of them. I felt uncomfortable because I have always been independent, and I still am.

I know blindness can take its toll on people who once had vision, but I did not realize that it can actually make people dependent upon others. I felt like I was in kindergarten because learning what I needed to know was very new to me and being around a bunch of crybabies was also very new to me. I know it may seem a little too harsh for me to say this, but it is true, at least until reality hit me hard. Then I realized that I was a scared little crybaby too, and now I know why others were crybabies. This is what I do not like about reality. When it hits you, it hits you hard.

You see, I never knew what it was like to be babied, not before school and certainly not now. I have always had to be the strong one with the backbone to hold up the world, and even though my blindness was a setback for me and got in my way, I still had to remain strong and persevere through any trial that came my way. I never gave up on anything without a fight, no matter how much vision I was losing. I still do not give up without a fight, even though I have lost almost all my vision. When reality finally caught up to me I came to realize that I was a human who made mistakes and that it was okay to make mistakes. I used to think that it was not okay to make mistakes because I always looked at my mistakes as a sign of weakness. I guess you can call it pride. My pride had set in for many years until reality hit me hard.

I used to think that that school was not for me. I thought, *Why am I here? I don't like it here. I don't want to be here, and I certainly do not need to be here. I want to go home, but unfortunately, I cannot go home. I now live here, and I am just going to have to adjust somehow some way. I am stuck here, so I am just going to have to make the best of it. It is so hard for me to be here because I miss my family so much and I am having the hardest time trying to accept reality, but I am dealing with it.*

I did not realize how comfortable that I had been until I moved to Seattle and started school. My whole life was surrounded by God—I practically lived in church—but now I was around others who did not worship God. Wow, it was a totally different world for me. I was not used to living outside of God's house, and now that I was, I have attracted so many enemies. My mind did not know how to adjust to the way the world thought because I was so used to thinking the way that God thinks. For God says not to live the world's ways (Romans 12:2). No wonder people thought that I was just too righteous for them, especially knowing that I strove to do the right thing every day.

I loved doing homework, and they thought I was abnormal. I always believed that knowledge is power, and they thought that it did not matter whether or not they learned. I was told many times by different students, "What is the point of learning? One of life precious gift is gone—vision." I was told that life was not worth anything without vision to see what it has to offer. But then I had realized that I used to think the same thing. I just never thought I would hear someone else say the same thing.

Does life ever get any easier? In my opinion, no. You see, living for God life just gets harder, especially when your faith gets stronger. The trials get harder and longer, it seems like. God called me to take a step of faith and step out of my comfort zone, and when I did, all hell broke loose! And therefore, God grants me the courage to face the unknown!

3

Courage to Face the Unknown

So, what does the unknown have to offer us? You can sure bet pain will be involved. But pain is not what we are to think about when we are faced with the unknown future. Pain is just the key to surviving the unknown. And it will certainly drive you through the unknown to face what is known to us. Now our future is in the unknown, and if you want to see what your future holds in store for you, you need to face the unknown with courage. For without courage, it is impossible for you to face the unknown and step out of your comfort zone to do it. God promises to be with us wherever we go (Joshua 1:9).

Here is the truth about me having to face my unknown future. As I have mentioned in my first book *In the Midst of Pain*, my daughter has filed charges against me about a false claim that I have physically abused her son. Well, for three years, I have not been able to see my grandchildren because there was a restraining order filed against me in the courts. As of now, I am able to see my grandchildren, but when I do, I am faced with the fear that she will blame me again for something happening to one of her kids. I do not trust my daughter, but God said that I am to trust in Him (Proverbs 3:5).

This is where the facing the unknown comes in. Should I allow the fear of the unknown to stop me from accepting all that God has for me? Because if I do, then that means that I am not trusting God with my future. Or should I face fear of the unknown with courage and trust God to turn what is meant to be evil into something good for me. I think the second choice is my best opportunity. God has made a promise, and God is not a god who fails to live up to His promises. I do believe that I need to trust Him to take care of the evil influences that try to destroy me. Thank you, Lord, for reminding me that you are the only one in control over the things in my life!

As I slowly begin to let go of my fears that my daughter will bring evil against me again, I have been more open to wanting to get closer to my grandchildren. I now have four. At the time of the accusations, she only had two children, and the last two she had nine months ago. The children are now eight, five, three, and nine months, all boys. None of my grandchildren know me except for the oldest boy, and he only remember the bad things that were said about me, and that is a shame. It has been very hard to try and restore my relationship with the oldest boy, but the others are still young enough that it will be easier to have a relationship with them. I just hope that my daughter does not hurt me again, for I do not think I can handle anything drastic from her again.

It took God to pull me out of the pit of hell that I was feeling, so I believe that it will take God to get me through these years to come. I do believe that God has plans for my life. His plans are to prosper me and not harm me (Joshua 1:8).

I know that deep down in my heart God is asking me to let go completely of all the fears that can hold me back so that I can put all my heart and trust in Him only. God does not want me to be afraid of what could happen or what might happen. God wants to show me what He will do for me. But I need to let go all the way and trust God with all my heart because if I do not let go of my fears and trust God, then I will miss out on the most important opportunity of my life. I believe this is a turning point in my life, and I also do believe this is a very serious test of faith that will change my life forever in a positive direction. And I do believe that God is there for me and He will not leave me. God will turn my life to the good. Oh, amen to that!

Though I know it seems difficult for me because I am a human being, I know that with the help of God, all things are possible, especially for those who believe (Matthew 19:26). I trust you, God! And I know that you will use my fears as an opportunity to let me see better the life that you have given to me to live and to help me live faithfully according to your will, for it is your will that I choose to live and not my own. God, I know that I cannot do this without you, and I just want to say thank you for being there for me and helping through these painful trials in my life.

God wants me to make sure that I most definitely do understand that He will not ever leave me or forsake me and that He will always keep me in His thoughts (Hebrews 13:5). God wants me to remember that saying from the *Footprints in the Sand* poem. For God says that when I see only one set of footprints, He did not leave me. It was then that He carried me. When I was weak, God was strong, and so God has turned my weaknesses into strength, strength to take my failures and turn them into opportunities.

So now is my opportunity to trust in God with all my heart and move forward in life. God has promised me that everything is okay. God is asking me to let go of my fears completely, so as of right now, I am. Thank you, God, for always being there for me and working things out for my good! For I know that you are a God who always keeps His promises! Amen to that!

I also have come to know that my daughter does love me and that she really misses me too. She has missed out on all the holidays, birthdays, and family outings with me and the grandchildren for the last three years, so that also helps me to let go of my fears too. She also misses the thought that she used to have time out for herself when I would take the kids for a while and for overnight visits. Apparently, life has been rough for her in the last three years. She talks about not having any time for herself, and I know that she does miss me being there for her when she needed me.

I do give thanks to my good Lord because I do know that everything will turn out for the good. Now in this next chapter, I talk about how courage will destroy any fear that may come your way, for fear cannot dwell in a place full of courage. Courage gives you the power to wipe out your fears. I hope that as you read this next chapter, you will gain insight on courage, and I hope it will wipe out any of your fears too.

4

When Courage Destroys Fear

What does courage actually mean? Well, the standard college dictionary explains it this way: "the quality of the mind and spirit enabling one to meet danger of opposition with fearlessness, calmness, firmness or bravery." And the Bible dictionary explains it the way that God intended courage to be—"to have confidence, boldness and trust." For example, courageous people risk their lives to do what is right. And courageous people will also risk their reputation to do what is right. No matter what the consequences are, doing what is right is a courageous person's focus point. A heart that cares about what is right is better than a heart that is full of pride.

So now what does fear mean? It is an agitated feeling aroused by awareness of actual or threatening danger, trouble, dread, or terror. It means being scared or timid. It is an uneasy feeling that something might happen contrary to one's desires! For me, I define fear as being just the opposite of having courage. Fear will paralyze you, but courage will set you free to do bold things and accomplish whatever it is that you have set your heart and mind on doing. Fear will hold you back while courage pushes you forward in life. Courage is never afraid of anything.

But here is the problem. If you are not careful about the choices that you make, then fear and courage can both destroy each other. If you choose to hang on to your fears, then courage will not take root in your heart, and therefore you will always live your life in fear. You have to let go of one in order to retain the other. You cannot have both at the same time. Either you choose to allow fear to dominate your life's decisions or you choose to allow courage to dominate your life's decisions. You have to choose one or the other. Now as for me, I choose courage. Remember, life in itself is a choice!

For those who put their trust in God, God will give them the courage they need to face the evil darkness of this world. Fear will no longer have its place in your life when you trust God. For God never gave us a spirit of fear, but His spirit of love and power to conquer fear (2 Timothy 1:7).

Courage has pushed me through the barriers of fear that has tried to stop me from living a life pleasing to God. When I put all my trust in God, then my courage becomes much stronger than I have ever imagined. I have also developed more faith because I notice I now have the courage to face my fears of letting go.

The courage to be mentally and physically strong against the odds is an admirable quality in a person. And the person who has high self-esteem, perseverance, willpower, and courage to stand strong in the midst of their trials of pain will survive the unknown with confidence, knowing that they will succeed in their dreams and their goals. They will not let anything stand in their way of achieving whatever it is that they have set their minds on doing.

Courage builds faith, and they both go together because faith will build courage too. You cannot have one without the other! Except for one thing, faith is the substance of all things hoped for, and it takes courage to be patient and wait for it. Courage is the driving force that will allow you to make choices that fear would have never allowed you to make. And when you know that you have faith in God, then nothing becomes too impossible. People who live in fear live in pain, and therefore, they are unable to see life and live it for what it really is. Life is a very special gift given from God, and He expects you to live your life according to His ways without fear, not your own way. For God says not to let fear control you (Isaiah 41:10). Life itself is an unknown mystery!

I have learned to live my life for God the way that He expects me to live it. And therefore, I have learned to love and respect myself just as God does. With God's help, I have also learned how to respect the pain that has been bestowed upon me, and therefore, I have learned to accept God in a more valued way. For I do value the life that is given to me. And each living day, I acknowledge just how precious life really is to me. Thank you, Lord, for teaching me how to value my life!

Love and respect can teach a person about the value of life in general. For life in itself is a lesson to be learned. A person has no knowledge of their values of life until they first come to grips with it. Life is not meant to be wasted but made to be cherished with an honest heart to love and to be loved. So please just love, honor, and cherish this gifted life that God has given you to value. Make it your heart's desire! And may the good Lord bless you as you do! For the challenges of life's mysteries will deepen your faith in God, allowing you to overcome your obstacles. In this next chapter, I will talk about how fear can paralyze your courage to persevere through any painful trial that you encounter along life's journey. It will take a lot of courage to persevere through the most difficult challenges that life brings you, so take heart and do not lose courage (Ezra 19:4)!

5

Fear Will Paralyze You

AI have mentioned in my previous chapter that fear will paralyze you if you let it. Well now, I have decided to not allow fear to be in control over me and paralyze me. As of right now, I choose to face all my fears head-on, with my faith fully entrusted in God, for I do know that God will see to it that my fears will vanish. I will come out as a winner and not as a loser. Praise God for that! I choose to take the most impossible and challenge my faith in God! God has always been there for me through all my years, and I know that He is and will be there for me for the rest of my life. I trust in God, who has saved my soul from going to hell. I am very confident in God that all things will work out for my best interest (Romans 6 :28).

Now fear is very painful, believe me, for I have felt enough of it to know how it feels and what it can do to a human's soul. Pain will rip apart a human soul, but pain also has its way of healing the body and the soul. My pain has ripped my soul so far apart that pain is the reason why I am closer to God. Pain will have a heavy influence on you. And pain will either kill you or make you stronger at dealing with life's issues. Pain has made me a better and a stronger person. Pain has also brought me wisdom to understand why it is the way it is and why we have it. Pain also helps me to acknowledge that I am only a human who makes mistakes and that I need God to help me correct my mistakes and learn from them.

No when it comes to a comfort zone, well, unfortunately, pain will drive a person out of their comfort zone and into the unknown zone. Pain will help you to focus on what needs to be done. Pain drives you closer to God. It did me. Pain will also drive out fear. Fear will make you desperate to find the answer you have been looking for. The fear of pain will actually become the fear to live. God has promised me an abundant life, so I will not be afraid to live. I know that someday I will pass from this world, and when I do, I want to make sure that I am in right standing with God, for God is the only one who is in control of my soul. Every one of our days is numbered, and each day that I live is another day closer to my death! I want to acknowledge my purpose for my life each day I awake and then live out my purpose each and every day that I wake up. How about you? Have you found your purpose in life? Jesus Christ is my purpose for living!

So don't let pain and fear be what stops you from living the life that God has blessed you with. Live for God and keep your faith in Him, for nothing is impossible for God to do! Live each day as if it was your last day on earth because you never know when you will reach your last given day. Remember that life is a very precious gift and life is very fragile. So take it one day at a time and strive to be the best that you can be.

6

Courage to Persevere

Courage is that one thing that people seem to lack these days, and they lack it the most during hard times. Well, it's either you do or you don't have it. If you do, then you will succeed at anything that you set your mind to. But if you don't, then you will fail at everything before you even start.

This is where my step of faith to have courage really begins at. On March of 2012, I started school at the department for the blind. Well, first of all, I had to move three hundred miles away from my family just to go to this school. And when I started school, I did not know how to accept my blindness. It took a lot of courage just to step up to the plate and go to school.

I will start with Braille. Braille was the hardest part of schooling for me because it is like learning a whole new language. Braille is just a bunch of dots, and each dot represents a letter. So, the memory part was hard, but the writing was a lot harder because you had to write everything backward. No matter how much courage I had and no matter how I kept trying to do my best, it was just so confusing. I just was not able to continue Braille, though I did complete grades 1 and 2, and I do know how to read and write Braille for the most part. Now, in home economics, I learned how to cook and cut things with a knife being totally blind. It was scary because I was used to cooking with sight, and now I had to learn to cook blind. It was hard because I did not know when something was done unless I timed everything or when the talking thermometer would tell me the temperature. But the cutting was easier because I would feel with my hand before I would cut. I cut celery, carrots, and onions. That still took some courage to do.

So now in mobility class, my instructor would have me to walk outside and down the sidewalk, and he had me walk across the streets without audio signals. The hardest part for me was to know when to walk at a crosswalk. The very first time that I had tried to walk across a very busy street with crossing signals, I was so scared that I just could not do it. Reality was setting in, and I did not like it. I just refused to accept the fact that I am blind. So I freaked out and started screaming for my instructor, and he assured me that everything was okay and that he would not let anything happen to me. Then I started to feel safe again. So my instructor just worked with me around small areas with hardly any cars until I was comfortable enough to cross the bigger streets that have more traffic that would challenge me.

Well, it took a couple of months before I realized that I was ready to cross the streets with heavier traffic. It took some courage, but I did it. I actually crossed a heavy traffic intersection blind, and when I was finished with my mobility walk, I was so proud of myself, of God, and of my instructor for teaching me. Courage is not to be taken lightly, for courage in itself is the key to your inner strength, and your strength comes from God. I even wonder at times if it takes courage just to have courage!

Then I had computers also known as ZoomText. I did not know much about computers or typing until I came to school. Now I know just enough to get a job. The hardest part for me about learning is the fact that I thought I was just too old to learn. I am only forty-six years old. The main reason I felt like that is because it was so hard just to learn what teenagers learn in high school. Back when I was in high school, I did not know what computers were or cell phones or iPods and iPads. Everything was old-school type. I had no idea what technology was back then. I just barely know now what it is. Anyways, I had class for four hours, which was difficult because I would get bad headaches, and then I would lose concentration. Then I would get frustrated and would want to give up, but thank God that I never did give up. God gave me the courage and the strength that I needed to persevere through the difficult times. God has promised us that He would give us strength (Philippians 4:13). I just took a break and took a couple of Tylenols and went back to work. Perseverance was very hard, but I did it with a positive attitude of knowing that I can do it. Keeping a positive attitude played a major role in perseverance. I stayed in constant prayer with God!

Now the last class I had was shop. That was a challenge for me. I thought my other classes were hard, but shop to me was the hardest and the most challenging of them all. Crossing a busy street was scary, but cutting wood was even more frightening. This is where it took courage to build my confidence. I made a baby cradle, and it turned out beautiful. Though I did have some help from my instructor, I walked away with confidence that I can do anything that I set my mind to, even if I am blind.

On October 26, 2012, I graduated with honors. My shop teacher was very proud of me, and my ZoomText teacher said that he had not seen anyone so committed as me in the seven years that he had been there. I was so happy to hear that. It really made me feel good to know I can achieve what it is that I would want to do. My cooking teacher said that I just did what I had to do without complaining and that she was proud of me because my cooking tasted great. And she also said that though I had many trials and hardships while in school, I still persevered through them and did not give up and that she was very proud of me for that.

Now as for my mobility instructor, he said I had a photostatic memory that just took him by surprise and that I also had a very good sense of direction. He said that he is very proud of me and that my hearing was so terrific, I could hear a pin drop on the ground. As a matter of fact, I did hear a leaf, just one leaf, blowing across the sidewalk with traffic going by. Wow, that is how good my hearing is. And in Braille, my teacher was still proud of me for learning what I did because I can still read and write in Braille. I had been in school for a total of nine months! And I have learned all this stuff. I now have a better life now, where I know how to get around better and do things for myself and for my family, especially cooking and cleaning.

Also in school, we have this one class on Tuesdays and Thursdays, and it is called seminar. In this class, each person had a topic that they could talk about. Some students chose not to pick a topic and also chose not to speak. Me, I chose to speak, and when I did, not too many people were happy or even pleased with me, but a few people were, at least. When I spoke, I would hit on a few topics that became too hard for some of us to accept. I was not like this when I first started school. Talking about my blindness was so difficult for me, and often, I did cry when I would talk about it. But as time went on and I was actually able to accept my blindness and talk about it, that was when no one else wanted to talk about it or even hear me talk about it. And then, in return, it became harder for me just to talk to anyone about anything. I certainly did not make too many friends while I was in school. Just a few liked what I had to say, and that is not much at all.

I just wanted to give up so many times and just walk away. I wanted to drop out of school because I felt that this school was not the place for me to be, and of course others felt that way about me too. But it took God to remind me that I am not a failure and that I am not a quitter. That was where I had to take a stand and keep my courage to persevere! I knew that I would soon have to face my fears. I kept on reminding myself that I was not a coward and I could not give up, for I knew that God was with me and God would see me through those problems. I just needed to keep my head held up high and keep my focus on God, not on what people say or think about me. I knew that God had a blessing in disguise for me, and I just needed to be patient and wait for it.

I have come to notice that life itself requires a lot of courage just to survive, and if you want to do more than just survive, then life will require of you to persevere through pain. But, unfortunately, too many people take the easy way out because they stayed focused on their weaknesses and not their strengths. Too many people give up when it comes time to push life to its limits. The more you push, the harder it gets! They let weakness take control of their life, and now they have no purpose in life. It is just so sad to think that people take the wrong choices in life, and it ends up costing them their life. So, the choice we have is either we can be a coward and give up, or we can be courageous and live a decent life. But just remember that it does take courage to persevere. Without that, we die from our own weaknesses. So what do you choose? They say that life is what you make it, so what have you made your life to be?

In my next chapter, I talk about our weakest moments of faith!

7

The Fear of Living

What does living really mean? Yes, we wake up breathing, but what does it really mean to live? How can a person take advantage of life while another person takes life for granted! So, what is the purpose of life, and what does it actually mean to live it? Do you think about your life and the purpose of it? Does life have the same meaning for a blind person as it does for a person with sight? How can we fully understand the meaning and the reality of life? For you, as an individual, how would you explain what the meaning of life is and what its purpose is?

Here is what *life* means in the standard college dictionary:

> LIFE: The form of existence that distinguishes animals and plants from inorganic substances and dead organisms, characterized by the properties and functions of protoplasm as manifested in metabolism, growth, reproduction. The characteristic state or the condition of an organism that has not died!

Here is what *live* means:

LIVE: To function as an animate organism, to continue in existence, to remain or persist as in the mind. To remain valid, or operative, to use something as one's sole or customary nourishment! To pass life in a specified manner, to live in peace, to lead or regulate one's life as in accordance with rules principles and to spend or pass time of one's present interest and importance.

And this is what *purpose* means: intention, aim, intent, object, motive, goal, reason, plan, driving force, point, etc.

Well, now you get a glimpse of what the dictionary says, but what actually is the reality of living your life and the purpose of your life? Just think about this for a moment!

Now here is what *life* means in the *Nelson's New Illustrated Bible Dictionary!*

LIFE: The physical function of people, animals and plants. In physical terms, life is the time between birth and death, because God is the source of life! Life! It is the ultimate gift from God! Life is more than just a physical experience life took on a spiritual meaning, often referring to the spiritual life that, results from our relationship with God! Eternal life is the highest quality of life and it means more than just eternal existence. Life is associated with light, gladness, fullness and active being. Death is contrasted with darkness, sorrow, chaos, emptiness and silence. To die is to breathe out one's soul and to revive is to have it return. Life and self is so closely parallel that to lose one's life means virtually to lose one's own self. Life is seen as something transitory, dependent of and at the disposal of God!

So back to the question, what does life really mean, and why are we living, or what are we living for? What is the actual purpose of life itself? How would you define what the purpose of your life is? When I went to church one Sunday morning, the preacher man said that the purpose of life is to glorify God, and I do believe that is true. Just think about it. What was the purpose of God creating us humans, and what was His purpose for us to live? Why do so many people fear life? They are so afraid to live their life according to their purpose, but why? Do you know why? As for me, I am still learning what my purpose is! I live with vision and blindness every day, and I still wonder what my purpose for living is. Does my purpose change because my vision changes? I am not sure about that either!

Sometimes I feel like I have lost my reason to live because I have lost my vision. Yes, I have visualized my purpose at one time, but now I can't see my purpose any more. Did I base my purpose on my vision? Yes. It is so hard for me to imagine what my purpose is being blind because I am no longer able to do the things I used to do. To envision my purpose is to envision it being blind! It's hard to envision something that you cannot see! How would you be able to envision your purpose in life if you were blind? Good question to think about! Here is something that I pondered on for the longest time about the purpose of my life.

On Sunday, April 28, 2013, my soon-to-be-husband and I took my friend out for lunch for her birthday. Now my friend is completely blind. As we sat down at the table to be served, she needed to use the restroom. So, of course, I am the one who had to take her, even knowing that I am blind too, though I am not completely blind yet. As I was leading her, I realized that I do not want to lose the rest of my vision. As I led her back to the table and sat down to eat, I noticed how hard it was for her to eat. I had to show her with her hands where her food was at and what food was what. It was so hard to watch her because I realized that someday it could be me doing the same thing that she is doing.

THE COURAGE TO BE BLIND

This really bothers me and really scares me too. So my question is, does a blind person have the same purpose in life that people with vision have? For me, I live in both worlds—the world with some vision and the world with more blindness. Right now I am trying to figure out my purpose for both of the worlds that I live in. For neither one is the same as the other! This is why I have fear of living. Am I living right, or am I living wrong? Although it has been said that life is what you make it and that you get out of it exactly what you put into it. Really! So then what does a blind person make of their life, and just what exactly do they put into it, or how can they put something into to it? Now that is a question to ponder! If only I knew!

So I am curious about something! I wonder if people with vision would have the same purpose in life if they were to lose all their sight! And I do not mean to say this in a negative or a harsh way. I am just curious to know! Yes, I know that there would be some things that would need to be changed! And accommodations would be needed to be able to get around and do things that need to be done. But the question is, would they still have the same purpose as to when they had vision? As for me, I am still trying to figure out that part because I still live in both worlds.

In God's Word, in Isaiah 55:12, He says, "For you shall live in joy and peace." So what does God mean when He says you shall live in joy and peace? What does He mean by the word *live*? Well, in the handbook of the Bible application, this is what *life* means: "each moment of life is a gift from God," and life is short no matter how long we live! If there is something important that we want to do, then we must not put it off until tomorrow, for tomorrow may never come. If you had only three months to live, what would you do, and how would you do it? Would you tell someone about Jesus? Would you tell someone that you love them? Would you deal with some undisciplined area in your life? So, don't neglect what is truly important in life, for you only have one life to live! Human life is very valuable in the eyes of God, so value your life the way that God does! It is so ironic that people spend so much of their time trying to secure their lives while here on earth and yet spend little or no thought about what comes afterward, when you pass from this life into the next. Accomplishing worldly tasks makes no difference in eternity, for we cannot take anything from this world with us when we die.

What makes life so valuable to live, and why should we value our life? And why does life have meaning? Knowing that you have vision, would your life be just as valuable to you if you were to go completely blind? I guess that would all depend on if your life is valuable to you or not! For me, my life is valuable! But I am just not sure how to fully live my life since I have lost most of my vision. My life is so different being blind! I am just trying to make it through each day, and I'm still trying to live out my purpose for my life—if I find that purpose, that is!

My friend who is blind has a different perspective on life, and when I talk to her, it does make sense. But for me, I want so much more in life. I am just not sure how to go get it. I live in fear at times when I try to go after the things that I so dearly want because I am always falling down and getting hurt or walking into things and getting hurt. I have fear built up inside of me because I am always getting hurt in one way or another. I know that I shouldn't live my life like this, but I do! And I am not sure what to do about it. When I try to reach higher for the stars, I fall harder. I feel like giving up at times because I cannot win for losing, it seems like. I know that people get like this even when they are not blind! I do recall a saying that living for God is valuable and living in the light of God's eternity makes my life of efforts more valuable. For God knows that I do try!

I do my very best to live my life according to the way that God wants me to live it. I do rely on God to help me get through these sad and depressing times when I am not sure where my life is headed! Being blind is so much more different than when I had more vision. It seemed like I had a lot more to live for back then, compared to what I have now. I was certainly more active, and I weighed less, and of course, I was not so depressed then. I am having such a hard time trying to adjust to the lifestyle that I have now, living in a blind world. Everything just seems to fade away too easily and too soon. Every day that I wake up, I am hoping and praying that I do not go completely blind. My children keep telling me to look ahead and keep my head up. And the best man in my life tells me that everything will be all right. And you know what? Jesus is so right! My husband loves me for who I am and says that he will always be here for me. He tries so hard to understand my blindness, but the sad part is, if you are not blind, then you will not understand. But I do give him credit for at least trying to understand. Well, this is what it is like living the life of a blind.

8

Losing Hope

It is hard losing all your hope and seeing the damage it then causes! What is hope, and why do people make the choice to either hang on to it or to give up on it? Hope is believing in something you do not have and believing you will receive what it is that you are hoping for (Hebrews 11:1). How would you describe what hope is? There are so many things to believe in and so many things to hope for, but why do people give up on hope? Have you ever really hoped for something, and when you did not receive what you were hoping for, you felt like you have set yourself up for disappointment, and you just wanted to give up on hoping for anything? Well, I have! I do not do it much anymore, but I used to a lot. For now, my hope is in the Lord and not in my own desires.

Losing all your hope can seriously cause a lot of damage to your soul. I have not lost all my hope yet, but there was a time that I almost did. If it was not for God, I would have given up on all hope for a better future. Now the hope that I did lose has caused me so much damage and pain that I realize that hope is all that I do have in the midst of chaos. People say not to get your hopes up because all you are doing is setting yourself up for disappointment if what you are hoping for does not come. Now that is actually true! But look at it this way, hope is where you put it and who you put it into. I put my hope in the good Lord, and if I do not receive what it is that I was hoping for, it is okay. I will not let it get me down because I know that God has a better plan for me, and whatever it is that I was hoping for may not be what God wanted me to have. So where are you putting your hope? What are you putting your hope in, and who are you putting your hope in?

Before I realized what hope really is and what the real meaning behind hope is, I have many times put my hope in the things that I thought that was important to me and the things that I thought that I needed the most. In all reality, it is God who I need. As long as I have God, I have everything that I need, and nothing else will do. There has been so many times that I have set myself up for disappointments because my hope was not in the Lord! Hope will always fail you if you do not put your hope in God. So what does hope actually mean? There are two ways people look at hope, but there is only one way that God says what hope is! Let's see how God says it!

Biblical hope is a confident expectation where there is belief in the living God, who will intervene in a person's life. God can be trusted when we put our hope in Him alone. Therefore, you cannot separate hope from faith, for they both are one. Hope is the anchor that penetrates deep into the unseen spiritual world of the human soul. Therefore, it will never disappoint you. Hope will keep you from being anxious about your future if applied with the right attitude. Hope helps you endure your suffering patiently and it helps you be a Christian whose hope is free from selfishness. Faith in God should be a Christian's hope and a Christian whose hope should be based on that. Jesus is the source of all our hope. To trust in Him is to put our hope in Him. For without trust, there is no hope. Our challenges are overwhelming, and unless you can see that God's purpose in these day-to-day challenges is to bring about the continuing growth of a Christian, then you will be in despair.

Pure genuine hope is not someone's wishful thinking! Pure genuine hope will assure you about the things that are unseen. Pure genuine hope comes from God and is given to the believer who will put their hope and trust in God. Hope gives us confidence in trusting Jesus Christ and eternal salvation. This is how a Christian has hope. So now what does the dictionary say about hope? A standard college dictionary says,

> HOPE- To desire with expectation of fulfillment, to wish, to want, to place confidence or to rely on! To continue hoping even though it may be in vain! And so vain means- Unproductive, worthless, fruitless, useless, having no real basis or worth and no purpose! This is why people set themselves up for disappointment. I like God's theory on hope. To hope for things that eternal, will last forever and one day it will come. When you put your hope in God and the things that are eternal, what you are hoping for will never be in vain.

There are so many reasons to believe and so many things to hope for! But, as for me, God is my reason to hope and the reason why I believe. If you put your hope in the things that will not bring you true joy and more abundance, then I believe your hope is in vain. Anyone can hope for anything in life, but if you are not careful of what you put your hope in, it will cause a decrease in your sense of human value. It leaves you in despair. Then you lose all hope and want to give up in life when the challenges become too difficult to endure, and your strength turns into depression.

In my life, I have had many hardships and challenges that have brought me so much pain that hope is the only thing I had to hang on to. But so many times, my hope has failed me because my hope was not in those things that God wanted for me. At one time in my life, my soul was so damaged that I wanted to give up everything in life because I thought what I was hoping for would be what would make my life right. But it wasn't. People cannot make your life right. Jesus Christ can. And that is where my biggest mistake was. That is why my hope was in vain. You cannot put your trust, hope, and faith in people and expect everything to work out for the best because people are humans, and people will fail you, but God never will fail you! People make mistakes, but God certainly never makes mistakes. Amen to that.

I once thought, *What is the point on striving for a better future? No matter what, it will not change my eyesight. I will still be blind!* But my life is not about living in darkness. My life is about living for God and seeking His ways for my life. God can and will still use me for His kingdom to be an inspiration for others! As long as I have God and I am seeking His ways for my life, then I will always have something great to hope for! Praise God for that! God has opened up my understanding to what hope is, and now I do realize that if I would have given up all hope, then my life would be so damaged that my soul would ache for life, or I would have been dead.

What can hope do for people? Well, hope gave me the desire to write this book, and I do trust God for the reason of this book! Having hope helps me to gain more insight on courage, and the faith of having at least some hope gives me something to hang on to in life. So why do so many people lose hope when faced with pain from life's tragedies, and why would some choose to give up all hope in moving on in life? Yes, of course, tragedies are very painful, but hope in God will pull you through any pain if only you choose not to give up on God. Hope in God has pulled me through some of the most intense tragedies in my life, and I know God will do the same for you! Just give God and His hope a chance to see what miracles will come your way. But you must remember one thing! Hope requires patience, and patience is a virtue. Patience can become very challenging. I face this challenge every day!

Many people including myself either lose hope or have lost hope due to lack of patience to wait for what it is that is being hoped for! That seems to have been my reasoning. But let's look at some other reasons. When someone is in a series of challenges, they want an answer right away, and they hope that they get it. It is so hard to be patient when enduring the pain and suffering that is involved. No wonder we want answers now, not later or tomorrow. Enduring patience under trials is impossible to do on our own, and that is why we need the grace of God to help us.

People seem to live in despair when they lose what it is that they were hoping for. This is when people need to turn to God and put their hope and trust in Him instead of giving up what they are hoping for. Believe me when I say that God will help you to keep your hopes alive, and only He will give you the true genuine patience you need to help you endure the pain. I am still trying to hold on to what hope that I do have left, and God is the one who is keeping my hopes alive through Him. The day that I lose all hope for a better life and a better future will be the day I am buried. Until then, my hopes will remain alive in God. It will only be death that ends all my hope. I guess this is how it is for many people!

When we look at our circumstances, we seem to get discouraged easily! And to face the unknown of our future makes it harder for us to hang on to the hope and face the reality of what is real. Often, people wonder if what they are hoping for is really real or not! Is hope real or just a figure of our imagination? I guess it would depend upon who believes that hope is real! Well, I believe that as long as we have God in our lives, then we have a reason to keep on hoping for what is not yet seen. This is why I said previously that it is God who is keeping me from losing all my hope and my faith in Him. For I know that I cannot live without Him! For it is God who has given me a better life to live, a better future! And He will do the same for you, I know He will! God is so good I would never want to live without Him ever! Amen to that!

When you put your hope in the things that can be seen, then there will be no reason to hope for something that is not seen. That is the whole key point of hope—to believe that you will have what you have been hoping for, even things that are not seen. Just think, without hope, life then would just be too plain and too easy to live. We need a sense of purpose to feel like we are a human being, and we also need to feel the pain of the things that we are hoping for. I believe that hope keeps the heart going in the right direction and searching for the answers that our human minds wonder about. Hope will cause a person to have courage to take the plunges of life and face the unknown future. And of course, hope will keep your mind going in a certain direction that will guide you to the truth of the matter and help you to search out for what is right.

What does the Bible say about hope? It says, "The happy anticipation of good" (2 Timothy 1:7, NIV). A Christian whose hope is based upon the fulfillment of God is being faithful to all mankind. When you have complete hope in God, your fear will diminish quickly. A person gains more insight on hope when they learn to walk by faith in God and not by the sight of man. When the time becomes too difficult and we are not sure of what to do, we can certainly depend on God and feel more of His hope for our lives, which will increase the power for us to believe that everything will be all right and that we have nothing to fear even if we do not see any results yet.

I have noticed that when I lose hope, it is usually because I have lost my focus on what's the most important in my life—God! My hope was never in vain as long as I stayed focused to God and all His promises. And now I do everything in my power and then some to stay focused on God. Though I do realize that it is God's power that I need! God grants me His wisdom and His power to keep me focused on Him. I know that there is just no way that I can do this on my own will, for I know that I surely need God to help keep me focused on Him and not the things of this world. The world has nothing to offer me that will give me something to hope for, not even peace of mind. So just keep the faith in whatever it is that you are hoping for because God will bring to pass whatever it is you set your hopes on. God has done this for me. As humans, it is just in our nature to lean toward the worst of our circumstances instead of relying on God to bring the good out of what is bad.

Now for us believers, we put our hope in Jesus Christ's return to earth. Nonbelievers have been known to put their hope in the things of this world. They put their trust in other human beings instead of God. A nonbeliever does not acknowledge God when they put their hope and their trust in us humans. Here is a good example: let's look at doctors. Yes, a doctor can save lives through medicine and surgery, but a doctor cannot and will not save a life that God chooses to take. It is God who puts breath into your lungs, and it will be God who will take that breath away on His time clock, not ours. That is the difference between a believer and a nonbeliever's hope—where they put their hope and who they put their hope in. It is so sad how the world thinks and what they put their hopes in. Now you must believe that a hundred percent genuine hope is not wishful thinking!

So when you are hoping for something, make sure that you start taking inventory of what your meaning is, because when you put your hope in God, then you will know that your heart can be at rest and that your mind will be at peace in the things that you are hoping for. I know that God will give you peace for your soul because he has given me peace for mine, and now my soul is resting in Him (John 16:33). For we all can count on God to be there for us when we are in times of desperate need.

Losing hope is easy to do, for I have been there and done it, and though I did not lose all my hope, I still lost enough to cause me hardship. I have, at one time, lost a great amount of hope that depression from losing what I once had in my life set in. Hope is a good thing, and that good thing is what I once lost. The more I stayed focused on all my problems, challenges, and circumstances, the easier it was to get depressed and want to give up! I realize just how easy it really is for anyone who faces life's difficulties to sink into a deep depressed state of mind and lose all their hope for a better life. Enduring the pain from losing hope can seriously rip apart the human soul!

Now here is the good part! I have experienced that when the time came for my head to be lifted up, God was always there to rescue me from my depression every time. He set my mind free. God has given me His reasons for His hope. God continues to remind me of His precious son, Jesus Christ, His death on the cross, His burial and His resurrection, and that is the reason for all this! So, what about those who do not believe in God? Well, the way I know it is that God loves everyone and sent His son, Jesus Christ, to die for all mankind. Those who choose not to believe take their life into their own hands and do as they choose to do with it. They will pay the price in due time for their unbelief. God has given humans free will to choose life or death. So, our life is our choice to make, and we certainly cannot choose it for someone else. But so many times, I wished I could.

The only hope that nonbelievers have is in their own selves because they think that they are the ones who are in control of their own destiny. I believe that this is why they eventually lose all their hope and end up in their graves earlier than expected. Premature death seems to set in all too quickly for the nonbelievers, and it is really sad to see all this happen, especially to our younger generation. There are way too many teen deaths happening because of people losing their hope in the things of this world. The world has nothing to offer us that is worth keeping because you cannot take it with you when you die. Not enough teens are being taught to put their hope and trust in God, and therefore, teen death rate is rising. Do our younger generations ask questions? I do believe so. But do they get the answers that they are searching for? In this case, who wouldn't give up hope!

In this next chapter, losing your hope can cause your faith to become weaker. Just remember, true genuine hope and faith go hand in hand. It is impossible to have one and not the other.

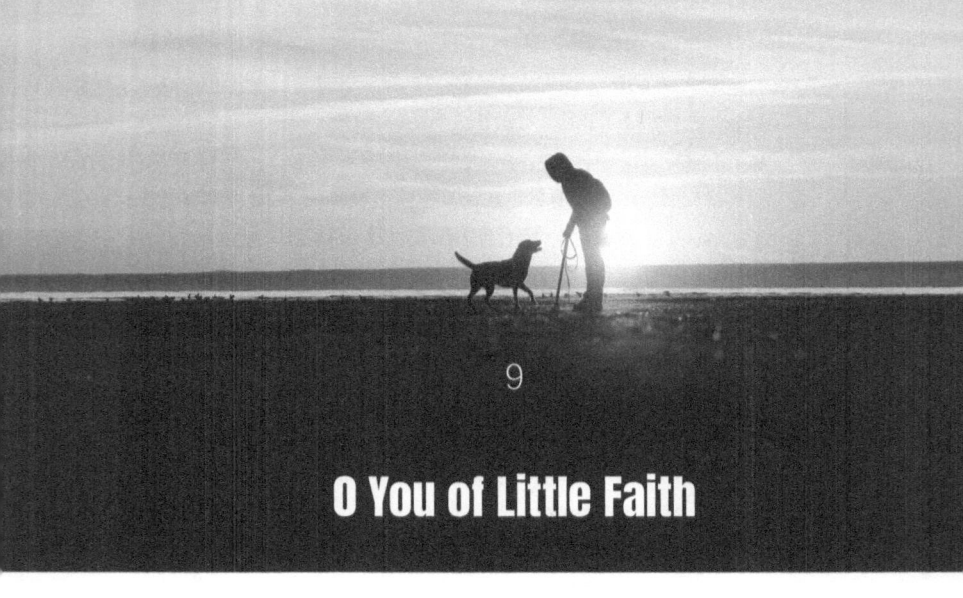

9

O You of Little Faith

In Matthew 14:31, God says, "O you of little faith! Where has your faith gone?" Too often, my pain has become so unbearable that I cannot even see through it or past it! My blindness is beginning to take a toll on me. This is how bad pain has become for me. It is so intense that I am losing any vision that I do have left. It's too unbearable to even think about it. So, for me, to envision any faith seems so impossible. It's hard to envision something that you cannot see! My pain has been so unbearable that it feels like a knife is cutting deep into my soul and just leaving it to bleed. Then weakness starts to eat at me! Oh, where is my faith during these painful trials that life has bestowed upon me?

Oh, if only I knew! Although faith is real, so is my pain! Oh, but if I could feel faith physically as I do my pain! How I wonder if my faith would be stronger! How much more I shall praise God during the midst of my pain and sufferings! Well, as we may know, faith just cannot be felt in a physical sense. It can only be known through one's belief that faith does exist, and it's only through pain that we may know that faith is real. So many times, I have fought for the things that I need and want. So, I need to fight the good fight of faith if I am going to win this battle to keep my faith (2

Timothy 4:7). I will fight for what is right and what is true! But so many times, my faith has been too weak to fight the good fight of faith. It is then that God gives me His grace and the strength to keep on moving forward and not to give up on the fight for my faith. This is when it takes God's grace to get me back on track facing life with faith head-on. For I know that it would not make any sense if God did not help me through my pain.

My faith is like my hope! During the midst of the deepest, darkest moments of my life, my faith becomes the weakest. It is only through God's strength that I become aware of the faith that I need to hang on to the most. When I fight the fight of good faith, I am actually fighting for what is right and true in the midst of painful circumstances that seem way too impossible for me to endure alone. It is God who has helped me to endure the pain with His faith!

Fighting the good fight means fighting for the things of God that are eternal, like love, joy, peace, forgiveness, and praying for those who hurt you! Yes, all these things are a struggle to get and to keep because it is not human nature to love our enemies and pray for them, and for a human to forgive another human for the pain that is caused just seems impossible to do. But God says that nothing is impossible for those who believe. Matthew 17:20 declares this. Even for a Christian who lives God's ways, it still becomes difficult to do. So when you fight for what is right, you fight with your mind and your heart, and you constantly need to ask God to give you the strength and the wisdom to do it. Without God, we will lose the fight.

So we need to take a stand for what is right and fight for our faith in God because God will see to it that we will win the good fight of faith. Praise God for all that! Our fight is between good and evil, and our war is not against other people; our war is spiritual (2 Corinthians 10:3-4). It is so easy to do the things that are not good for us, and it is so fun to do the things that are bad for us because that is our human nature. The most intense challenge about living life is doing what is right in the eyes of God and not in our own eyes (2 Corinthians 10:5-6). This is why the fight is on! But God gives us warnings. The more you fight and struggle for what is right, which is God's ways, then the more that evil will come against you. But God also reminds us that if we do not fight for what is right and live His ways, then we are doomed never to live a good life. And we will face God's consequences (Hebrews 2:1-3)! Ouch!

Evil corrupts our moral behavior, so when trials come, we start losing our faith. Evil has its way of telling you that you are weak and not good enough and even that you're too weak to keep living, so then you think, *What's the use striving for a better life?* Evil just tells us to give up, and so we do. We give up too easily instead of fighting for our faith in God. We let evil rule our hearts, and therefore, we lose faith and give up on what is right. Our hope is gone; it has faded too quickly! Have you ever noticed that doing the right thing seems to hurt more? It becomes more painful because it takes more effort to do, and it seems to be against what we were taught growing up as a nonbeliever or in a non-Christian-based home. Struggle to do what is right because just living itself is a struggle. We struggle to do what is right, and doing what is wrong does not require any effort from us; doing what is wrong is too easy to do. That's the human nature in us.

So many times, it has been so difficult for me to keep on fighting for my faith during the midst of my darkest moments. When there is no light in my life, then I start losing my hope. God, I need your light in my life to see where I am going. God guides me by His light, but my problem is that sometimes I will stop when He wants me to keep on going. This is when it seem to be the darkest moments for me! Many times, I just want to stop and take a breather because the pain is just too intense for me to move on. This is why perseverance is so crucial to keep. Perseverance makes it even harder to endure the pain! But, as they say, only the strong survive, so I must keep going if I plan on surviving this fight. I must lean on God's promise that He will be with me through all my pain and suffering and that He will give me His strength to carry on. I must believe! I will believe!

God says that He will never stop shining His light on me as long as I continue to follow Him! He promises to always be with me until the end of my time here on earth (Matthew 28-20). There is one thing for sure that I will take to heart, and that is that God will never lie, for it is not His nature to lie (Titus 1:2). God will come through with what He promises! Amen to that!

So how is your faith today? How are you holding on to your faith? Where is your faith, and who are you putting your faith in, God or humans? As for me, all my faith is in God only! And that is what I am holding on to! For only God can choose what He wants to do with my soul! And that can become a scary situation! I really believe that God is taking good care of my soul. I know that my soul is in His hands. I cannot give my soul to anyone else, and even if I could, then I definitely would not trust my soul with anyone! God has never let me down, and I do not think that He ever will! Just think about how your life is going right now and about what direction you are heading in!

Here is something for you to ponder! God says in His word (the Holy Bible) that someday we all will stand before Him and give an account for the way we have lived our life while we were here on earth (Romans 14:12). So, if you were to die today and stand before God, what would be your final words? And when you die, what would people say about you and how you lived your life? Would it be good talk or bad talk? What kind of life would you have left behind? Makes you stop and think, doesn't it! I know that I think a lot about my life and how I am living it from day to day! So, while you are alive and have the chance, you can choose to live right and know the truth of reality or live in wrongful disorder and listen to the false words of evil and reject the truth of reality! So please, think twice because you never know when your life will expire. There is always a choice to change the things that you can!

Just remember what the word *Bible* means (B-basic I-instructions B-before L-leaving E-earth)! Please never forget this!

Here is a prayer that keeps me in perspective. It's called the serenity prayer and was originally written by American theologian Reinhold Niebuhr. I've added my own thoughts to it.

> God, grant me the serenity to accept the things that I cannot change, courage to change the things I can, and wisdom to know the difference, but most of all, please, God, grant me the courage to never give up on what is right, even if it may seem hopeless! Thank you, God!

God loves you, and He wants you to make the right choices, but He will not force you to do anything you choose not to do. As for me, I fear God in reverence of knowing that my soul is in His hands. When I am in need, I choose to turn to God and not turn from Him. I cannot and will not run from God, for there is no place to run to anyways. To run from God is like trying to run from your own self. It's impossible to do. For every time you turn around, you are still there, and that is how God is. He is there no matter where you turn in life, and He will never leave you. So do you fear God, and if you do, do you run to Him or run from Him? You should think and meditate on this question!

When I run to God in prayer, He shows me so much of His mercy. He has given me so much peace from all my trials. God did not and will not remove my trials from me, but He does give me His peace to endure them! This might not make any sense to you, and it may not be what you believe, but it sure gives you something to think about and ponder for a while!

So what does *reverence* mean? And what type of fear does God mean when He says to "fear the Lord and keep my commands" (Deuteronomy 13:4)?

Reverence means to show respect, to show affection, or to stand in awe, as in reverence to God's holiness and righteousness!

To fear God means to have respect for Him, and God wants you to show Him affection. God wants you to stand in awe of Him, for His glory is amazing! So I really hope that you ponder and meditate on reverence for God in hopes that you will fear the Lord.

There is one thing for sure, and that is that life and death is nothing to mess around with! Life is the most precious gift from God, and death can be the most devastating if your life is not right with God before you pass from this life. The fear of living can cause you to lose hope. So please, make it right starting today because you never know when your time here on earth is up!

10

Enduring Perseverance

The pain of being blind is a disability that I have to endure for the rest of my life. The doctors say that there is no cure for my eye disease, which is called retinitis pigmentosa. And the harder it is to endure my blindness, the harder it becomes to persevere through it. It takes the loving act of God to get me through each day, and I thank Him every moment for it. Without God, I would have already given up in life.

You see, my dreams and goals are based on living for God each and every given day. I set my mind on the things of God and His plan for my life. But the hard part of living life is living my life being blind. For each day, it seems like the simplest little things become such a big task for me. And so many times I have felt like I am a burden to my family!

One of the hardest things that I am dealing with right now is how I am supposed to feel and act around my family when we are out doing shopping or just going places.

My children and my husband are always saying, "Watch out! Watch that step! Be careful, there is someone next to you," and then they pull me by the arm to move me out of the way. This is so hard for me because people need to watch out for me because

I cannot see them. It just seems strange to ask a blind person to watch out where they are going.

I went through schooling to learn about my blindness and how to cope with it, but my family still does not understand what I don't see and how I feel. I have a walking cane that is specially made for the blind, and the school has taught me how to use it. So I try and tell people that I can walk by myself, and if I run into someone or they run into me or even trip over my cane, I say sorry, and they say sorry, and the problem is taken care of. And most of the time people are usually telling me sorry. That is just how life works for us blind people. All too often people with vision do not understand what it means to be blind, and it is hard for them to understand a blind person's world.

But no matter what I say or do, this is what I have to endure for the rest of my life in order to persevere on this journey that I am on. But one good thing that I do have going for me is, I have God helping me to be strong and of great courage. God gives me the courage I need to keep on moving forward in life. And enduring perseverance is the most difficult task for me to accomplish.

I have no choice in life but to persevere and endure the pain that is bestowed upon me because if I choose not to endure my pain, then I will not survive for very long in this world. In the world today, only the strong will survive these cruel and evil last days that we are living in today. Life is hard enough for anyone to live in this world, but it is much more difficult to live in it being blind. For there is just too many cruel people out there who just do not care about anything in life, not even about themselves!

When you endure pain, it is usually for a good purpose. It is to change us to be a better people and to live with faith and courage so we can be a living testimony for others who are struggling to survive their pain. Some people are just too weak to endure their pain, so they give up life for exchange for an early grave. And of course, there are some who just do not want to endure their pain, so they try different methods to kill their pain instead of facing reality and dealing with it. This is why it is very important not to give up during the midst of enduring your pain. My purpose for enduring so much pain is to share the good news of Jesus Christ's death and resurrection on the cross in hopes that others will try and endure their pain as well.

Jesus Christ did not only suffer while hanging on the cross, he had to endure all his pain before he was even hung on the cross. Jesus Christ not only endured his pain, he also endured the pain from mankind, and He did it because of mankind—to save our souls from hell. Now that is what I call enduring perseverance. No human can ever begin to endure Jesus Christ's pain, or even imagine the pain that Jesus Christ had to go through. But, of course, what we do endure from our pain is bad enough!

So how much pain have you endured? How much pain made you want to persevere even more? Or have you given up? Or perhaps you are on the verge of giving up! Well, my friend, please do not give up, for I know that God has a plan for your life. The road gets very bumpy, and you might hit a few potholes, but you will eventually hit smooth parts. Life is not all about the bad things that happen to us. Just look at the good things that you do have and focus on that. The more you focus on Jesus Christ, the better your life will be, and the more understanding of your pain you will be. Jesus Christ understands our pain more than any human can!

So, what is it in life that can cause a person to break down? Then once a person is totally broken, what gives them the strength to endure, and why would they want to persevere? What makes some people strong enough to want to move forward in life no matter what it is that is making them lose their strength to carry on, and what makes others want to just give up in the midst of their battles in life? What makes one person different from the other? We all have flesh and blood and a heart with feelings. We are all human beings, but why would some remain strong and some remain weak? What makes us that way?

I know that we are all different from each other, but what is it that makes us so different from one another? Is it the way that our parents raised us that makes our beliefs in life different from others, or is it just because another person just makes you the way you are and you feel like someone else is responsible for the hardships in your life? So what is it?

To me, life has two different worlds—a world of pain and hell and a world of life and blessings! I live in both worlds, but if I stay focused on God, then I will live in the world of life, love, peace, and blessings that only God can and will give me. You see, I believe that each person can choose what world they want to live in! As that old saying goes, "Life is what you make it," and I truly believe that! No one else can make your life the way you want it to be or make your life the way it is. If you want your life to be full of love and blessings and peace, then you need to form a relationship with Jesus Christ. For without Christ, we have no life, except a life of hell and pain. And for some reason, so many people would rather choose this type of life instead of a life with God. I believe that this is why the world is so full of pain and agony!

So the ones who choose to move on through their pain and persevere are usually the ones who know that there is something bigger and better than them out in this world that can help them through their trials and their pain. This goes for nonbelievers too. I believe that when a person's soul is in pain, they start searching for answers. But too many don't want to know why, and they choose not to search for answers. Their pain is just so bad that they give up and just want to die because they think that death is the answer to ending all their pain. They just do not care to look for a reason to live because their pain is so intense that they cannot see past it or see any way out from it. I believe that those who are searching for a better way in life through all their pain will be the ones who seem to persevere in life! So, what do you think? As for me, this is just what I believe and think.

I have endured so much pain in my life that at times I wanted to give up. But there is a part of me that is so strong that I cannot and will not give up. My soul keeps me searching for the right answers. And as long as my soul is still searching, I will always have the endurance to keep on persevering. And that, my friend, is what I call enduring perseverance!

God is with us all to the end. For me, enduring perseverance helps me to see courage in my darkest moments! So, what steps have you taken to develop perseverance?

11

Seeing Courage in Darkness

This chapter is unique. It is about being able to see courage through my blindness. Now I am not totally blind yet, but I am severely low vision-impaired. I have very little central vision left, and I have no peripheral vision at all. Well anyways, this is about me and my mobility instructor while I was in school for my blindness and learning how to live all over again—this time with little vision.

This chapter is unique because my mobility instructor had not met anyone like me before, and he was curious if I was faking my blindness. Actually, he thought that I was just lying to him. So, I had to prove to him that I was not lying to him when I said that I could not see. Each time I went on a mobility walk with my instructor, I had to wear sleep shades. These are glasses that are painted black so you cannot see through them. Anyways, each time I had walked with my instructor, he would think that I was cheating. He kept on asking me if I can see anything at all with these glasses on, and I kept on telling him no because I couldn't. He said to me that when he wears them, he can see around the outside of the glasses, and I said, "But I can't because I have no peripheral vision." He still did not believe me. He told me numerous of times that either I was cheating and lying to him or I was just really good at what I do. I said, "I know what I am doing, so I must be pretty good." I also told him that I do not walk by sight, I walk by faith. And I said to him that when I walk outside, I pray and ask God to guide me, then I release my worries to Him and walk by His guidance, and if I am good at what I do, this is the reason why. But my instructor did not believe me. When I spoke about God guiding me, my instructors reply was, "Wow, okay. Well, if that is what you think helps you, then okay." It was different trying to tell my instructor why I was so good at walking with no vision. Now this is not just a story. This is real life. I really do trust God, and I really made a lot of people stop and think, even though they did not believe me when I told them that God helps me. This really did happen!

So each day this would go on, and finally, one day my instructor decided that he would give me a surprise test, and I am so happy that he did. I passed it with flying colors. Now my instructor wanted me to use his shades that are called Mindfolds. Now these are big fat huge black glasses that have black foam all around the eyes. He said, "I know you will not be able to see out of these glasses because I can't!" So I put them on, went outside, and did the usual, except he mixed up the streets a little bit to try and throw me off course. But that did not work because I still knew what I was doing. Now to my surprise, he had two other people with vision come along and watch me, and they were so amazed at what I could do. "It's a miracle," they said. When we got back to the school after the surprising journey of a walk that we were on, my instructor decided to apologize to me. He was in shock that I could do things without vision and that I was not cheating or lying to him. From then on, he treated me with respect. He has also commented that I am really good at doing what I do! He never doubted me again; when I say I can do it, he believed in me, although for some strange reason, he does not seem to think much about God having anything to do with me being this good. And I do pray that someday he will come to know God, and maybe then he will understand me and everyone else like me.

Now as the story goes, these are the things I did with the help of God, for without God, it would have been totally impossible to do the things that I did. Here is one of those things that I did. As I was walking down the hallway blindfolded—that is, with my black glasses on—I walked right into the room that my instructor asked me to go into, and I did it without bumping into any walls or the doorway. He then asked me, "How did you do that?" I asked him what he meant, and he said, "You walked right in the room without bumping into the sides of the door." And I said that God guided me. I also told my instructor how the door was lit up around all the sides.

He didn't understand, and I said, "You know, when a room is engulfed with flames, and you are on the other side, and you can see the sides, top, and the bottom lit up, and it looks reddish yellow." When he said yes, I told him, "Well, I said that is what I saw. And that is how I knew it was a doorway and how I could enter it without touching anything."

He said, "Wow, okay." But for some reason, it seemed like he did not believe me. You would think that he would have by now.

Well, this kept on happening each time he would ask me to do something. My instructor finally told me that I had a sense of direction that he had never seen before, even with people who are totally blind and have been since birth. Well, guess what? *That* is the power of God. What an awesome God we serve. Amen to that.

Then their came a few times when I was on my walks with my instructor, and I would stop and say, "Did you hear that?" And he would ask what. Then I would tell him, and he would ask me how I knew that. And I had told him that my hearing is very good, in top condition, and because I learned to trust God in the things that I need to hear for when I am walking blind. All my instructor would say is, "Your hearing is amazing!"

Then I had what is called a drop-off. My instructor drove me to this place, and he drove around in different circles to confuse me, and then he drove me down the street and said, "Okay this is where your stop is." So I got out of the van, and he drove off. I had to find my way back to the school in one hour blindfolded. At first I was trying to remember where I could possibly be. I knew that God was with me and that my instructor was somewhere near watching me; he'd told me that he would be. I started to get scared, but I remembered what my instructor had taught me. I knew that giving up and quitting was not an option for me as long as I knew I had God to turn to for help.

Well, as it turns out, the more I focused on God and thought of the things that my instructor has taught me, the more confident I was feeling. And guess what? I made it back to the school in less than thirty minutes. Wow, my instructor was so amazed, and some of the other teachers were speechless. They just could not believe that I have done it in that time frame. They just shook their heads.

Then I went on what they call a monster route, which is where your instructor gives you three or more places to find in one full day of school time frame. Well, my instructor gave me four places. He said he was going to give me five, but he was not sure if there would be enough time. So anyways, the day begins at 9:30 a.m. on October 22, 2012. I traveled to down town Seattle, Washington, which is a very large city of about a half of a million people. I traveled to each place, and I lost my instructor twice, and he had to call me and ask where I am at. Then he said, "You are a fast walker, and you are certainly not afraid to go anywhere, are your"

And I said, "No, I am not afraid. As a matter of fact, I love walking. I walk all the time in Seattle, the place that my instructor and other people from the school have told me to be very careful about, especially when walking in the downtown area because there are a lot of crazy people out there who can hurt me, especially with me being blind. But nothing stopped me because I have God with me, and I trust in God 100 percent. And when I tell people that, they just give me weird looks. I feel so sorry for people who don't know God and the miracles He can do for them!"

Well, I reached my last stop and still had a few hours before school was over. My instructor said that he should have given me five places and wished he could've. Then he said that I can go ahead and go back to the school without him because his day was finished, so I went back to the school without him.

When I got back to the school, the teachers already knew what happened. They said that my instructor said that I did a great job and that he could not keep up with me. Everyone was happy with me. That made my day. My student advisor said that not too many students do four places in the short amount of time that I had finished. And so now they are all pleased with me. They said that I was a person who loves a good challenge. Yes, that is me! I love challenges, for what is the purpose of life without any challenges? To me, challenges brings you to a newer and a higher level in life, and when I pass the challenge, I feel like I'm on top of the world, like I can conquer anything through Jesus Christ, who gives me the strength to carry on (Philippians 4:13). And when I am faced with a challenge, the challenge helps me to face my fears with confidence. Amen to that. Thank you, Jesus.

I am so grateful that God gives me the strength and the courage to wake up each day and face each new challenge that comes my way. God's challenges help me to put my trust in Him more, and challenges strengthens my relationship with God and Jesus Christ even more.

Now here is the exciting news. I did graduate from the Department of the Services for the Blind school on October 26, 2012.There is only one thing that bothers me. For some reason, it seems my instructor did not like me very much, and I think it is because I talked about God and the things that God does for me. My instructor just seems like he is thrown off by my response to his questions. No one there talks about God except for me. And the most difficult part for me is that when I did speak of God to anyone at that school, no one wanted to hear about God. Quite a few students would judge me and ask me if I thought that I was better than them. They felt like I was, but in all reality, I was no better than them. I am just a person who has a relationship with God. I love God with all my heart, and I am not afraid of what people would think when I talk about my Lord Jesus Christ who died for me. And I give God praise for that.

Even though I may be blind physically, I still have vision spiritually. God gives me His eyes to see through and His ears to listen. For nothing that I do is done on my own free will. I know it to be a proven fact that I can trust God with all my heart in any circumstance that comes my way. For I know it is God himself who gave me this heart to believe in him. God did come through for me with every promise that he has promised in His word. God never has and never will let me down. I believe I can go anywhere at any given time for any given reason and know that my God is by my side all the way. I will not be afraid as long as I have my whole heart and all my trust in God. I also believe that what I do have others have the same opportunity to receive the same blessings. For I know that I am no more special than anyone else. I just have a relationship with Jesus Christ Himself, and I have *love*. Amen to that. Thank you, Lord, for everything in my life that you have given to me.

And now for me to see through my blindness, I have written my next chapter "Visual Blindness."

12

Visual Blindness

What does blindness look like, or what is it supposed to look like? How does a person with vision know what blindness looks like on a person? The only way to be made known is with a blind cane, black glasses, or a guide dog. But what does blindness look like on someone who is visually blind?

Often, I hear people say to me, "Oh, I forgot you were blind and that I do not look like I am blind, and they even say I do not act like I am blind until they see me run into something or someone. Blind people get around good, sometimes even better than people who have all their vision. People with vision are not aware of their surroundings due to the fact that they often do not pay attention to what is going on around them. For a person with vision, this is very easy to do. A person who is blind has no choice but to slow down and pay attention to what is going on around them, because they cannot see what is around them! But that all depends on if that person has not given up their will in hopes to live a better life. Me, I am living my life in hopes of inspiring other people, and since I have been in school for my blindness, I am learning how to live again!

I can get around without my cane if I walk very slow and hold my hands out to the side of me to feel what is on either side of me. Without my cane, I have to constantly be looking down when I walk, but with my cane, I can walk a straight line looking ahead or looking at things on either side of me. I feel more comfortable with my cane because I get around better and faster, although I still run into things at times!

There has been so many times that I thought my life was over when I realized that I was going blind and that there is nothing the doctors can do about it. But I realize that I am very blessed to have such a good life of blindness because I am now working at a public library. I put books in order and put them on the shelves. I have to walk without my cane because I am pushing the book cart, and that is why my coworkers forget that I am blind. They say that I get around really good and that I am a happy person. But I was not always a happy person.

Before I had recognized and accepted my blindness, I was always depressed and wanted to give up. I always knew I was going blind, and each day just got worse, but it was when I had finally accepted my blindness that I became free to be a happy and a blessed person. My pain and my blindness has brought me closer to God, and now I know that there is nothing impossible that I cannot do as long as I hold on to Jesus. I praise God for all that has happened to me. God has brought me to a whole new level of thinking.

Pain has opened my eyes to understand that life is a very beautiful gift that God has given to me, and I am blessed to be alive and to be an inspiration to other people who are experiencing some form of pain in their life. If it was not for pain, I would not have gain the insight that I needed to survive living in a dark world.

This is what courage is all about. For me, pushing life to its limits and then beyond took so much courage and the faith not to give up when I got lost. Though there was no light to be seen, I know that God is there guiding and inspiring me to keep moving forward. God promises me that I will reach my goals and succeed. My inspiration will help many along the way. And therefore, I see the blind side of the truth! That is why I wrote this next chapter based on blinded truth. The truth can be interpreted wrongly.

13

The Blind Side of Truth

It was a dreadful morning when I woke up, and I was certainly not looking forward to going to school today. I had already had it set in my mind that I would probably be kicked out of school because of all the problems that I am having. I am having a very difficult time trying to adjust. I just don't think that school is for me! I am not used to being around a lot of blind people. Instead, all my life I was around people with vision. This is why I had such a hard time accepting my blindness! I do not know how to react around blind people, especially when we are in the hallway and we run into each other. I am used to bumping into people, but I am certainly not used to people bumping into me, especially head-on. All my life I have known for people to watch out for me. But blind people cannot do that!

Now one of the biggest problems that I encountered while I was in school was that they would depend on me to do things for them because I do have a little bit of vision left. At first, this did not bother me. I was happy to help. But then it became an issue for me because it got too hard for me to do everything, they depended on me for. But when I stopped helping them, they would get upset with me, and then the problems would begin. But the whole point of being in school was to learn how to be independent and not to be dependent on others.

Then the other problem I had was that I would get a lecture about helping the other students. I was not supposed to do that. This whole entire blind thing got to the best of me! I just do not like being blind! Now, although I still have a very little of vision left, the department for the blind says that I am still blind. They wanted me to accept that fact that I am blind, even though I can still see even if it is just a little bit. The point was that they are trying to prepare me in case I do go completely blind, and if I did, then I would know what to do. Well, I guess they have a point! At least I can say that I know what to do now. But no matter how much training I had, I will still never be prepared to lose the rest of my vision completely. Nothing can prepare me for that!

I have noticed something different about being blind! I am reliving my childhood days. I remember, for example, the times that I needed my mom to be there for me without worries! I remember her taking care of me, making sure I am dressed and ready for school, doing my laundry for me, making dinner for the family, keeping the house cleaned for us, and taking me to the doctor's when I needed to go. I get so scared sometimes that I feel like I need someone there to help take care of me. I hate feeling like this because I am so used to being independent. Now I feel like I am losing my independence, and that really bothers me. My job is to take care of my family and not have them to take care of me! When I was in school, I have seen so much of this in other blind students. But some of the students liked it, and some were like me. They did not like it because of how it made them feel about their life in general.

I believe that in some way that it is our human instincts to have that natural desire to want the world to feel sorry for us, no matter how strong or weak we are. We all have them downtime days, when all we want is the world to be handed to us instead of us striving to get it. And, yes, being blind does make it easier for us to be dependent upon others. Although it is no excuse, we do it anyways. I have found myself in that situation, and I do not like it. I also do realize that whether I like it or not, it is very easy to do without realizing that I am doing it. I don't realize how dependent I can get on people until they say something to me about it. My mind tells me that life just gets too hard to live being blind, so therefore I start relying on people more and not acknowledging it. Help! What do I do to stop doing this?

The reality is that the more I become dependent on people, the less I learn to do things for myself. This is just not me! I was never like this before I went blind. And what is even harder for me is when I tell people no thank you for their help, they help me anyways, and some people even insist that they help me or do something for me instead of letting me do it. People think I will just get hurt. Yes, that is true, but how am I supposed to learn to do it for myself?

Now for those who do not have the proper training, their blindness can and will be a hindrance for them. I know exactly how difficult it is to be blind and have to live in a world of people with vision. Life being blind is the most difficult challenge that I ever had to face, and it is a never-ending challenge; each day just seems to get harder and harder. But that's life!

I have had proper training when I went to school, and yet I still cannot adjust to being blind. I have noticed that quite a few students were like that too. I guess my blindness is not so much the hindrance as failing to accept my blindness is. I realize that I cannot accept my blindness because I still have some vision left. How can I be blind if I can still see? Well, people ask me the same question. This is why I wrote visual blindness. I have had my vision for quite my whole life, and for my brain to think different is a serious challenge. When my brain picks up signals that my eyes can see, it becomes almost impossible for my brain to think that I am blind. This may not make sense to you, but in reality, your brain is a computer, and it only operates what you tell it to. You cannot type something and have the computer tell you different. That is how my brain works with me. When my eyes see something, my brain registers what it is. But yet when I cannot see anything, my brain shuts off, as if it went to sleep. My brain cannot be in two different places at once and expect the same results!

Now as I approached school, I had to take a deep breath as I had started walking into the students' room. This is where all the students would meet before school would start. When I entered the room, there was complete silence, so I thought that it might not be a bad day after all. Then there was this one student whom I had tried to talk to, but she didn't want to talk to me, and then she asked me to leave her alone, so I did. At this time, I knew something was not quite right. Now for the life of me, I just could not figure out why this certain student did not want to talk to me, and nothing made any sense to me. I had done no wrong to this student, and I did not even know her. Well, I finally figured out that you do not have to do anything wrong for people not to like you. Some people are just miserable and do not like life, so then they probably will not like you. Their problem does not start with you. It starts with them, but they want to blame you anyways!

Well, I came to find out this student was upset because she thought I was wrong for not wanting to help those who were in need and can hardly do things for themselves. This totally just blew my mind, for I am not a miracle worker. I have a hard enough time trying to take care of myself and trying to learn what this school is teaching me. I could not possibly do everything for others who do not want to help themselves. I just could not believe what I was hearing!

Then the principal came in and said to me that she needs to talk to me, and I asked her if we could hold the meeting for another day because I was feeling overwhelmed with anxiety and I wanted to talk with a clear mind. But the principal didn't care because she had to address the meeting now, and she insisted that I be there.

So, I had to meet with her after lunch. This really got to me because I just knew for sure I was getting kicked out of school because of too many complaints against me. Yes, I quit helping people. Now they think that I am being selfish and mean to them, and so they started complaining about me. But I have noticed that they did not help me when I asked for help. They just thought I had enough vision to do for myself. Wow, really! Life is just totally unfair don't you think so? But, oh well, I still have to live in this world and face the hard-core facts of good ole reality!

I was dreading this meeting so bad that I could not even eat. It took a toll on my mind so much that I just literally started crying, and then I ran out the door, and I felt like running into the street just to get hit by a car. But God was with me, and He instantly brought to my attention His grace and how sweet it is. So, then I started praying, and then I was singing, "Hold me Jesus, cause, I am shaking like a leaf" And wow, it was so cool that God intervened, and I had so much peace and the confidence to face the meeting with courage. I never thought it would of turned out so good. God turned the evil talk into good thoughts from the principle and the teachers. Now after talking to God and feeling at peace, I went back into the school and went on with the meeting. But to my surprise, my counselor was there, and she defended me and my honor.

She honored me because I went by the rules and applied myself to the program and tried to get as much as I could out of it. She said that I am one out of a lot of students who really is trying hard without wanting self-pity. And she said that this is why I am having so many problems with some of the students and that it is mainly the students who don't want to try and help themselves. My counselor said that she was very proud of me. Wow, that totally made my day, I did not get kicked out of school, and God turned everything around to the good for me. Thank you, God, for your peace, which surpasses all understanding (Philippians 4:7)!

To me, this school felt more like some kind of camp than a school. People were allowed to sleep in class, and if they chose not to do their homework, it was perfectly okay. Me, I chose to do as I was supposed to, but really, it did not get me anywhere. When I think about all the hassles I had to go through, I can definitely say this school was not worth my time. I feel like I have wasted nine months of my life that I cannot get back, and all for what? Just because I thought this school was right for me. Well, obviously it's not. I am still blind, with very little vision.

Also, when I would speak about God, not too many students or teachers, liked it. Some just flat out did not believe in God, and others just didn't care what God has to say. You see, I am a God chaser, and I totally love my Lord. I will talk about God anytime, all the time, every time anywhere I go! Though I do have respect for others, I do keep it to a minimum. This is the hardest school that I ever been in, and it seems worse than kindergarten. I just can't believe how I was really treated in this school. Even the children in Sunday school at church were treated better than I was in blind school.

During my time at this blind school, it felt like I had no right to be myself. I was supposed to be like everyone else because this school is about being blind and not about being yourself. The more I tried to be myself and be normal, the more the students thought that I was just too righteous to be in this school, and the students did talk about me like that. They even told me that. So, it became very difficult for me to learn. It seemed like I was too busy trying to justify that I am not a bad influence and that I was there to learn how to live again since I had lost almost all my vision. I tried to tell the students that I was not trying to think that I am better than them but that I was trying to better myself in order to survive in this world being blind. For some reason or another, they just didn't seem to get what I was saying, and they just didn't care about what I had to say about myself. They are going to think whatever they want to think about me, and I could not control their thoughts, or even make things right, unless I brought myself down to their level and their way of thinking and acted just like them. Now that is the one thing that I could not do because that is just not me or how I live, for I am a very independent person, and I love to worship my good Lord Jesus, and I will never stop doing that no matter what the world thinks of me. Amen to that!

Another problem that I had is that the more I would try to succeed, the more I had enemies, and the more they would try to keep me from succeeding. So what is so strange about this? When I spoke with the doctor who counsels the blind, he was informing me that there are not very many students like me who really try hard to succeed. When students come to this blind school, they are usually very depressed and feel like they have no life to live because the most precious gift, which is their eyesight, was taken from them.

You see, people do not realize what they have or how important what they do have is until the day they lose it all. I thought about this for a long time, and you know, it is so true. Do you ever think about everything that you have and how precious it is and what you would do if you ever lost it all? It's not too often that people really stop and take the time to do an inventory of themselves and the life they are living so they do not realize the precious gift of vision that God has given them. You know that saying "What the good Lord gives, the good Lord can also take"? People, please start taking inventory of yourselves and see if there is anything in your life that you may be taking for granted. Please do not wait until it is too late and God decides to take it away. Just take a good look at what you do have and be thankful for it and give God the praise due to Him, okay?

Out of all the students, there is this one new student who stood by my side and hugged me, and she is the one who loved to hear me talk about God. It made her feel better and more at peace. I really thank my good Lord for putting her in my life because if it means that only one person wanted to hear about God, then one was better than none. And that one made a big difference in my life, and I think I made a difference in her life too. To me, she is the one reason why school had a meaning to it. We helped each other through the hard times, and together we made a difference in each other's life. To me, that was worth it!

So as time passed, I was finally able to get back on track and finish school. I graduated October 26, 2012. I was happy that I did graduate, but I was sad that I had to leave my friend behind. I also felt more at peace after I graduated because I no longer had to deal with these people anymore. It is sad to say this, but it is true. Though I did learn some of the other things that I so desperately needed, it was hard for me to learn. But I did not give up on my schooling. I just kept on pressing through and persevering. Though I did succeed. I am so happy that it is finally over. I can say now that I can live again since I had to learn how all over again.

Now to understand the mind of a blind person, I have written this next chapter to explain what it is like to live in two different worlds and how these worlds can cause so much pain when they collide with one another.

14

Images in the Mind of a Blind

As mentioned in the previous chapters, how does a blind person see without looking? This may seem a bit awkward, but I am proof that this does exist. For I have experienced it for myself when I was in school for my blindness. Although I have very little central vision, I am still considered blind. While I was in school, my mobility instructor would blindfold me completely before we went on my journey of walks. Now considering that I still have some vision left, this became quite a challenge for me. Though my instructor said I have a sense of direction, I still got scared of where I was going, knowing that I could not see a thing.

The first time we got back to the school, I walked right into the classroom without touching the sides of the door or anything else around the door. I knew exactly which room I was in without counting any of my steps to get there. My instructor asked me how I just walked in like as if I could see. I told him that I had a vision in my mind of what the door looked like. But he said that all the doors look alike, so how did I know this was the one? I then told him about what my vision looked like in my mind. I have seen all the doors that were on this side, and I knew it was the first door that I had to enter. My instructor was very amazed.

He told me he had not seen anyone like me. But the sad part was that my instructor thought I was cheating and looking through my blindfold.

So as time went on, I kept doing the same thing, seeing things without looking at them. So, then my instructor decided that he was going to challenge me to see if or not I was cheating. So, he asked me to put on his blindfold glasses because he said that if he cannot look out of them, then he knew for sure I would not be able to see either. So, I put on his, and guess what? I couldn't see a thing, and yet I did the same thing as I have done with the other blindfold glasses. He then just said that I am very good at what I am doing and that I have a great sense of direction and that my hearing was miraculous. Yes, I do believe that it is a miracle, for how could I have done it!

This is the image I have seen in my mind. The hallway was completely black, and the door I entered was outlined with a glow, as if it was outlined with fire. And I told my instructor that God has lit up the doorway for me. And to this day, I do believe that!

I have noticed that when I am completely blindfolded, my brain automatically switches over to my other senses. My memory, hearing, and smell are very much aware of my surroundings. It is just a natural instinct that we pick up. But, unfortunately, it is only for those who pay close attention to their instincts. I have seen some totally blind people who could not do anything because they did not pay attention to their other senses, and some blind people just refuse to pay attention because they fear the unknown of what they cannot see.

Now, for me, I fear of what I can see in the known. I do not have the same type of fear when I am blindfolded. Being blindfolded completely makes me more aware of my surroundings because I do not get distracted by the things that can be seen when I am not blindfolded. For what vision I do have left is just enough to get hurt with. I am always getting hurt because my eyes tell my brain that I can see. But when I am blindfolded, my eyes cannot talk to my brain; only my other senses can talk to my brain. I hate living between both worlds—the world of vision and, at the same time, the world of blindness! My brain is too busy getting mixed signals, and that is why life is such a terrifying challenge to take on every day.

The mind has no fear of what the eyes do not see. Fear is only *false* evidence appearing as real. This is why there is no fear in the eyes of a blind. The blind eyes do not see the evidence of anything appearing to be real. For what the eyes do not see, the brain does not know. But, unfortunately, this will only make sense to a blind person; it is only a blind person who is able to live in both worlds.

15

Living in Both Worlds

I live in both worlds—a world that I can see a little bit but also a world where I am not able to see things around me. I have an eye disease called retinitis pigmentosa, which means that the retina is deteriorating. I have no night vision at all, and in the dark, I am totally blind; everything is black. I also do not have any peripheral vision or depth perception. But when there is light, I have some tunnel or central vision left, not much though, I have just enough to get hurt. In my right eye, I see only part of my central vision, and my right eye is almost blind completely. I rely more on my left eye, and in this eye, I see only tunnel vision.

The doctors say that there is no cure for my eyes and that someday I will be totally blind. They cannot give me a time frame. But I do know that as long as I hang on to God and trust in Him, I know I will keep what vision I have. As a vision-impaired/blind person, I often think about my life and how precious it is. I also think about how precious my eyesight is. And I do wonder that if I do lose all my vision, would I give up on life and lose all hope, or would I persevere through life's most painful challenges? What would you do if you were in my situation?

As for me, I keep telling myself that I would keep on persevering through life's painful challenges because I know that as long as I trust in God, God will not let me give up. He promises me that He will be with me and help me through all the pain. I have learned that life is a very precious gift! So don't waste it!

When I am in the dark, it does not bother me to think about my blindness because I am used to it. I know the pattern of my home, and I can get around in the dark. But in the daylight or when there are lights on, I am so accustomed to seeing the things that are important to me, and I know that if I lost all my vision, it would bother me because I do not know the layout of this world. When I am outside, I know where I am going because I can see, but if I were to lose all my sight, I would not be able to know where I am going when I am outside, for it is a very big world out there, especially for a blind person. A blind person is not familiar with any of the places that they are in because everything is all the same color—black.

A person's brain will remember what it can see, but a blind person's brain only remembers what it hears, touches, smells, or tastes. That is the only thing that becomes familiar to a blind person. There is so much to see in this world that a blind person misses out on. And me, I know I would miss out on a lot more than I do now if I were to go totally blind. So I just praise God for what vision I do have left and hope and pray that I do not lose the rest of it. This is a time in my life that I do realize that challenges bring me a lot of pain. Then reality sets in.

16

Challenges Bring Pain

Challenges, life is so full of them. Life brings us so many different types of challenges, and unfortunately, challenges bring a lot of pain with it. There is no such thing as challenges without pain.

Now although there are many different types of challenges, there are also different types of pain, with different levels. I pretty much have experienced them all. Here are some different types of challenges and pain and their levels. I will start with blindness.

Blindness is a disability because it becomes very difficult to walk, cook for yourself, work, take showers, and take good care of your basic needs, but if you have had some training, then it is not as bad, but it is still difficult. For example, when you are crossing a street, you really need to focus on your hearing, but the challenge of that is if your ears are plugged because of a common cold. When a person is blind, they have to totally rely on all their other senses, and they need the proper training to survive; otherwise, death comes too quickly.

Now there are other challenges, like being mentally challenged or having no arms or legs or hearing (deaf). No matter what the challenge is, there is still pain involved. I am mentally challenged and physically challenged. My physical challenge is my eyesight, and my mental challenge is post-traumatic stress disorder, depression, attention deficit disorder, and anxiety. I have a very difficult time trying to stay focused to the most important things in life that I need to survive. I have to take high doses of medication just to stay in touch with reality. And my blindness makes it more difficult to pay attention. Because when I do think about my blindness, I sink deeper and deeper into depression, and therefore, I lose focus a lot! Life itself becomes so hard to live just because of all the challenges I have to face each day I am alive, and it does not get easier; it just gets harder.

Now the pain level depends on the challenges. The harder the challenges, the more painful life becomes. I have never had an easy challenge! Have you? I guess that is why challenges are called challenges! So let's beak the word *challenge* down and see what it means to be challenged!

The standard college dictionary explains it like this: to claim as due, to demand a contest with, an invitation or dare to participate in. And the handbook of the Bible application explains it this way: we can expect the world to challenge our faith, and God will give us challenges too. Challenges will bring a person to their knees to help them to seek out God.

You see, to me, challenges are like taking a test. You are being tested to see if you can accomplish what is challenging. Too many people fail at accomplishing their dreams and goals because they turn away from anything that will challenge them to move forward in life. Why do so many people do this? I believe it is because they do not want any more pain to be bestowed upon them. And to me, what is the point of living life if you do not have pain caused by challenges? Pain will let you know that life is real. Challenges also help you live a better and more fulfilled life, a life with a sense of purpose. Challenges give you reasons to live, even though we may not understand the reasoning. Challenges are also a way to heal the human soul when your soul is in pain. Challenges will give people a sense of direction, and as long as you have a sense of direction and a purpose to live, then let your challenges be your opportunities to experience God's blessings upon your life. So please, just enjoy the painful challenges because there is beauty in disguise waiting for you to reach out and grab a hold of it. So just do it. You have only one life to live, so live it to the fullest and do not cheat yourself out of the life that God has given you.

My friend who passed away died with sadness in her heart because she did not really know how to live her life for God. When I spoke with her about Jesus and how much that God loves her, she cried. She was not bitter or angry toward God, but she did not fully give her heart, her mind, and her soul to God completely either. She had given up hope, and it seemed like there was nothing I could do for her except to pray for her. She did listen to a Christian song, but it just seemed to have made her more depress and sad because the song was so true about the way she was living her life.

Now my heart grieves for her because I do not know what is going to happen to her soul. Her fate has already been sealed, and now she cannot change her mind and ask God to forgive her. She cannot come back to life and live her life differently. But, as for me, I can learn from her mistake. I can live for God now, before I pass away. I will live His ways now. I am making changes that will benefit me and help me be in right standing with God. My faith in God keeps me alive with a special purpose to love for.

I look forward to the challenges of life, and I am ready to tackle the pain that challenges give me. I am ready to move forward in life and be a blessing to other people. I want to prepare my life to be an inspiration of hope to others so that they may have hope. I want to live my life to the fullest and push life to its limits, and I know that God is with me through it all, and I know that God will never leave me nor forsake me.

Now that I have found peace through accepting the pain of reality, I first had to learn and then endure the pain that reality gives. I speak of the pain caused by reality in my next chapter!

17

When Reality Becomes Painful

Sometimes we forget that pain is part of reality. Our pain is too great that we cannot even identify what reality is, even though our pain is real. This is just another way to escape reality. Reality is just too painful to accept! So here is the truth!

When reality becomes too painful to endure, people will always find ways to escape it. Why do they? Because reality is the truth of something that is real! So why do people want to try and escape the truth? Because some believe that the truth hurts! Yes, I believe it does! But to escape the truth hurts worse when reality slaps you in the face and you have nowhere to escape.

People find ways to escape reality by medicating it, or they will just lie about what is real so that they do not have to deal with the pain that reality causes. A coward will bury the truth and try to hide from it while a person of courage will dig it up and face it by accepting the reality of it. Dealing with reality with sober judgment can be just as painful, but at least you will feel the benefits that God gives, and your soul will be set free. People do not often acknowledge that the truth cannot be hidden from God. The truth will come back to haunt you until you admit it and face it. Trying to escape the truth is like trying to escape reality. There is no such a thing because life is real, no matter how one looks at it and deals with it. Nothing in life will ever be hidden from the sight of God. So the question is, how are you going to deal with the truth of reality?

It is very easy for people to slip into denial! It's human nature. All too often, we take advantage of our human nature, and the consequences of denial eat at us. But for us blind people, we often try to step out of those comfort zones, where we are used to having others do things for us. And you would think that telling the truth would be easy because we do not have to face anyone or look at them anyways. But the consequences are still just as bad because guilt will take over in us.

Sometimes people just want to curl up somewhere and forget they exist! But that will not work for me! I have tried it. To me, there is still too much of life to live, and of course, my kids and husband will not allow me to just curl up and not exist. They keep me active—too often. But I do thank God for giving me such a blessed family that loves and cares about my well-being.

Now for my brother, he does not have the support that I have. Instead, he drinks his pain away so that he does not have to face the reality of his blindness or the reality of life itself I have tried to help him, but it is even hard for me to pull myself up, much less to try and help him. I can honestly say that I know how he feels when it comes time for living your live in a dark world. My brother seems to find security in a numb mind until the numbness wears off. Then reality sets in again. Then back to his drinking he goes again! As for me, I turn to God for my comfort and peace of mind! God really does comforts me and tells me everything will be all right, and then my heart feels so much at peace with my soul. Now I can rest my mind in knowing that everything will be all right, for I have God with me. Thank you, Lord!

What is a comfort zone? I believe that it is a place of security from the fears and troubled storms we have to face in life. It shelters us from our pain! It is a place where we can choose not to face reality and feel the pain from it! So many people stay in their comfort zone because they feel safe there and because it is a place that they are familiar with. To move out of the comfort zone means that you are moving into that place of the unknown, and then fear sets in. Reality is that place of the unknown, and when you try and escape reality, you are really just moving back into what is known as your comfort zone. The fear of facing reality is real.

Some people do not like facing reality because they fear what pain can bring them. The pain is just too painful to endure, so back to our comfort zone they go.

The question is, are people really at peace when they are in their comfort zones? I am talking about deep inner peace of the soul! People might feel comfortable in their mind and body, but are they at peace? Reality is the world in which we all live, and there is no escaping it! I have found my comfort zone in Jesus Christ, for He has given me true genuine peace in my soul and not just in my body.

As long as I have God in my life, I have a sense of belonging in this world. As blind people, we are very vulnerable to life's biggest challenges. Therefore, we are being challenged on a daily basis to face the unknown in the future that God has in store for us.

18

Finding Peace through Reality

As I have written in my first book, *In the Midst of Pain*, one of my chapters was about facing reality and of how painful it can be.

When people are in the midst of pain and suffering, we do not often acknowledge that we are in the midst of facing reality. Reality is so painful that all too often we neglect to see the reason for it. The pain becomes so bad that we try and find ways to relieve it. Alcohol and drugs seem to be the answer many people find. But is it the truth for our answers?

Alcohol and drugs just deceive us into believing everything will be all right, but it will not bring peace to our souls! But reality can bring the peace that is needed if taken in the right perspective with a positive attitude. If we choose to face reality with drugs or alcohol or any other means for security, then the reality of it becomes more painful. And the truth is, there is just no way of escaping reality or the pain that is caused by it.

As I have also mentioned, it takes courage to face reality and step out of your comfort zone. When facing reality head-on, it can cause such a painful act that we refuse to move forward in life. The pain that is left to endure becomes damaging to your soul, and you are in a constant battle of a raging war between peace and pain.

We wage war against ourselves. Peace comes when we let go of what we cannot control and to change what we do have control of.

One of the biggest issues of pain is caused by the fear of the unknown. Many people will not step out in faith and take on the unknown with courage! When peace comes our way, we take on the unknown without fear, and not realizing we are doing it. Peace will give you the ability to do things without fear, and sometimes without even thinking about what to do or how to do it. You just do it. Peace will also give you a sense of boldness to take on big challenges and expecting positive results. Nothing will hold you back when you are at peace with yourself and God and the things that God puts in your path.

I have experienced peace in my soul at the hand of God's mercy that He had for me! Here is what happened. I did not deserve God's mercy, and I should have gone to jail instead. But God loves me so much, and He knew my most desperate situation that He gave me His mercy instead of jail.

Years ago, me and my husband, who was still my boyfriend at the time, were fighting, and he had been drinking. We have had so many fights due to his alcohol that I could not take it anymore. I cried out to God all the time, and for some reason, it just seemed like God was never listening until this one certain night that I came very close to injuring my boyfriend. And just when you think that God is not listening, He shows up and does a miracle in your life that will turn your world upside down.

It was a cruel and cold day! Me and my boyfriend were seriously arguing and fighting over his alcohol problem; his alcohol problem was so bad that he was dying from it. My life was spinning out of control so fast that I finally hit rock bottom. I have literally had enough, so I tried to end it when I had lost my mind. Seriously, I was not in the right mind to think of the consequences of the mistake that I was about to make before God had rescued me.

In the heated argument, I was going to hurt him, but thank God that I did not succeed in hurting my boyfriend when I had tried to end his alcohol problem. All my boyfriend said was, "Go ahead, I don't care." Now, here is the miracle. And here is the most awesome part. I felt a warm, peaceful, "deep down in my soul" type of feeling that I have never experienced at all in my life. I dropped the weapon and walked away feeling this warm sense of peace that everything is okay. Now I totally went from an angry attitude to an instant peaceful feeling. No human can do this alone, for I know within my heart that it was the hand of God's mercy on my soul. God gave me a chance to acknowledge who he is and a better life that He has planned for me. God came to my rescue. So, I packed my belongings, took my kids, and left him instead of hurting him. Thank you, God, for coming to my rescue!

Now, peace was given to me without me ever letting go of what was keeping me in bondage. I really believe that God will intervene in situations that are out of our control. This is why I do believe that if it was not for God's hand of mercy being on my soul, I would have been in jail or dead. When God says that He has a plan for your life, believe me, He does. I would not be here right now writing this book if God did not have a better plan for my life!

There is something that I need to address about this chapter. When a case like this happens to you, you need to be careful about how you would explain what happened. Because people, especially the one you are aiming at, will think that you are crazy. I tried to explain my circumstances, but I was still considered crazy. The reason people think that is only because they may not have a relationship with God and understand the things of God. The thing that I need to admit is that my relationship with God was no relationship. But I still believed in Him. The only reason I knew this was an act of God is because no human, not even me, can do any of this on our own. It is impossible for the human mind to think about good and evil at the same time and feel peace in the midst of their storm.

So, think about it this way, the next time you are angry, try to be at peace and drop your anger instantly and see if you can do it. I know that I cannot do it unless God is helping me. Though there have been many times in my life that God did not help me, and I was left to face the consequences of my own actions. Ouch, that is painful!

There had been many times that I thought that I was going crazy because one part of me did not know what the other part of me was doing! And trying to come to grips with reality was just impossible, because reality at the time was not real. Now, no one has to be on drugs or alcohol to be in this frame of mind. This state of mind comes from a hole that is in your soul and that you cannot repair on your own. And this hole only gets deeper and deeper the more you try to fill it with anger, lust, greed, and jealousy.

When God laid His hand upon my soul, that deep dark hole was instantly filled with peace, a type of peace that no human can fill. Alcohol and drugs would not even begin to fill that deep hole. And ever since that day, I have never been the same! God has changed me and made me a better person for who I am today. And God can do the same for you too.

I am so grateful that God will intervene when we least expect it, especially in desperate situations. No person could ever intervene the way that God does. I remember a few times that I have been in other fights and God did not intervene, other people intervened instead, and guess what? There was no peace, my heart was still racing with anger for the other person and I was left facing the consequences of my actions. Not so cool either! Now I live to tell the story of a God who rescued me from the pit of hell on earth.

Just believe in God and trust in His ways that He has a plan for your life, and God will show up and rescue you like He did with me. That is the most precious and peaceful feeling that I ever had, and no one can take that away from me. Thank you, God, for loving me and rescuing me from my own death. Oh, amen to that.

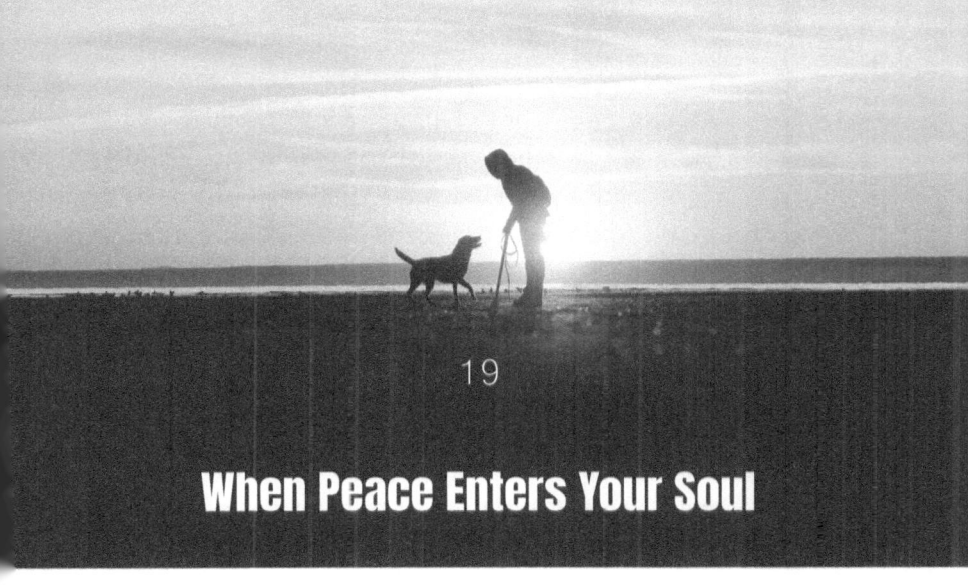

19

When Peace Enters Your Soul

Through all the painful trials that I have endured, I finally now can say that I found rest when peace finally entered my soul, and it is such a warm and peaceful feeling. I found God in the midst of my hiding place. When the storms of life came against me, God was there surrounding me with His arms of peace. This is such a beautiful peace to experience in a lifetime.

Has there ever been a time in your life where you just felt like giving up totally and you have finally hit rock bottom? You just keep on feeling this urge that there is more to life than what you have. And you wonder when you will ever feel at peace with yourself. Well, my friend, peace will come when you let go of everything that is weighing you down in life!

Peace finally came to me when I decided to let go of all my hurt and anger that was stored up inside of me through the years. It felt like I was drowning in my own web of sin, guilt-ridden, angry, and hateful attitude. All these years I kept searching for something that would keep me afloat instead of drowning me. And peace was, and still is, that floating devise. Without it, I would probably be dead from drowning in my own sorrows.

Now there are two types of peace. One will give you a temporary feeling and the other will give you pure and long-lasting relief. The one that gives you a temporary feeling just happens to be what the world offers. Like drugs and alcohol or just a friend trying to comfort you. And then you have the truest and the purest one of them all, and that one is the peace of God that surpasses all understanding. The peace that I have is a precious gift from God. Now God's peace will never give me a false sense of security. God's is all perfect and true.

The greater part about having the peace of God in my soul is that my soul will never go to hell, and I know I will rest in knowing that I have the peace of God holding my soul in the palm of His hand. Thank you, Lord, for that!

The more I live in peace, the better I can live life to the fullest, and I know that I can live out God's will for my life. God's peace allows me to peacefully walk confidently knowing that I am going in the right direction in life and the hand of God will always be upon me.

Do you know just how beautiful peace feels, especially in the midst of pain, when you are going through the toughest battle and you just don't think there is any way out? Well, there may be no way out, but you can sure experience the peace of God. God may not take away your pain, or make your toughest battles easier, but God will give you His peace that will help you through your trials and sufferings. God's peace has given me the courage to move forward in life and the peace of knowing that He is in my life with me and that I know that I can rely on Him for everything in life. I know that God will help me get through the most difficult battles that life throws at me. God prepares me for my future.

Often we may not know what our future holds for us, but by understanding God's ways and listening to Him, He will help us to understand more and help us to get a good glimpse of our future. For there is definitely one thing I do know for sure, as long as God is holding my future in His hands, my future is awesome. God will never start a good thing in your life without finishing it.

Once God starts something in your life, you can certainly count on God to finish it. Jesus Christ is the author and finisher of our lives. This is His promise that is in His word. The Holy Bible! God never lies and He will never let you down. Amen to that.

Many times, I still wonder what the future has in store for me, and I may not know just what it is that God is doing in my life, but I do know it is something wonderful. All the evil things that had happened to me will be turned into the good on my behalf, and I know this for sure because God made it a promise too, in His word.

I will be speaking more on this subject in one of my other books called *"Restored Hope!"* God has restored so many things in my life that people had tried to destroy, and I am happy to say that God came through on His promises and I am happier today than I had ever been. I praise God for that. Is there anything in your life that God has restored or that He is restoring right now? We serve an awesome God! When God restores your soul and everything that was done to you out of evil, that is "when peace enters your soul."

As peace enters my soul, God is unfolding a miracle for me!

20

The Unfolding of a Miracle

In this chapter I will speak about my painful past that I had with my enemy so you may understand how he became my blessing. Nothing good comes out of a relationship until something bad has happened first! God has promised that He will turn what is meant for evil into the good, and all things work together for the good. I truly believe this. Please read this chapter with an open mind because this evil man who once was my enemy is now one of my greatest blessings created by God's miracle.

On March 23, 2013, I truly saw God's miracle unfold before my eyes. It was our grandson's birthday, and it was so warm and beautiful outside. As we all celebrated, my daughter was taking pictures when her father said, "Hey, take one of me and your mother!" Wow, my mind drew a blank for a moment. I thought to myself, *This is the man who has been my worst nightmare for twenty-five years, and now he is being caring, like he is sorry for all the pain he has caused me. Then he put his arm around my waist. Wow, this is very strange because this is just not the man of my worst nightmares who has caused me so much pain that I wanted to die.* But, of course, I am talking about my past.

My past with this man has been such a horrible life for twenty-five years. The only reason I am living to tell the story is because we both have a twenty-six-year-old daughter and four grandsons in common. In my first book, *In the Midst of Pain*, I talk about my past life with this man and the struggles and hardships he put me through. This was the only man I have ever met in my life that was so cold, cruel, and evil. Believe me when I say that people can get downright cruel and hateful. Because they can!

Things are really different now that we are friends. But believe me when I say it is all of God's doings. The only thing I did is keeping up with my prayers for him. I have experienced such a warm and great understanding of what God means when He said that we are to love our enemies. For I know that I could not love this cruel man without God helping me. It is against human nature to love our enemies. All we want to do is to get even with the ones who severely hurt us. That is why I have a waging war going on in my soul. My human nature wants to fight against the things of God. Not cool.

Now that I have peace, I can honestly say that I have been blessed.

21

Feeling Blessed

Today I was at the park just enjoying the day with my family, when a lady said to her son, "Move over to your right a little bit, son, there is a blind lady coming through." Then she stopped and said to me, "My son has a cane too because he is blind." Now, I was wondering why her son was crawling around on the ground. For he was blind, and it was the only way he could feel his way around on the toys. I am glad the lady asked me about my blindness because she talked to me about her son who was ten years old. She said her son just went blind last year, he did have vision, but now he doesn't, and she said that the doctors do not know why he went blind.

Then I told the lady about my eye disease called retinitis pigmentosa, and she said she has heard of that, but that is not what her son has. I asked if he was a diabetic because diabetes will cause blindness unexpectedly, and she said no, he was not even sick. So, we shared our stories of her son learning Braille and me learning Braille too. It was quite an interesting story. After watching this child, I realized how blessed I am to have what little bit of vision I do have left.

People often do not realize just how blessed they are until they see someone else in the same situation. And even then, people still do not realize how blessed they are. As for me, I do realize just how blessed I am, and I thank my Lord for that. Thank you, God!

I quite often take inventory of my life, and I still wonder at times where I am going. I still take the wrong turns in life and ended up on dead ends. I guess that is the story of my life. I was watching that blind little boy searching for his way and yet not know where he is going. He had to rely on his mother to help him get around the park. It was really sad to see this little boy, but on the other hand, it was a blessing because it showed me how precious the gift of life is and it helps me not to spoil the gifts that God gives to us. I often think about the people in this world, how people just walk around with no purpose in life. They just wake up and live the same day over and over again and nothing seems to change. People are aimlessly living, and sometimes they do not even know why, and others are just too busy to want to know why. How often do people stop and smell the roses along their way in life? Not often enough! The world is so full of people who just don't care.

How often do you think about your life and the direction that you are going? Do you have a sense of purpose in life, or are you wandering around aimlessly, trying to figure out where to go? Or do you just go without thinking? Do you think about how blessed you are? What has God blessed you with today? I am blessed just to be alive, how about you?

The blessings of God are so amazing, but it hurts me to see people take life for granted, until they lose something that is important to them in their life! I look back at the mistakes that I have made, and I realize that I am who I am today because of my mistakes. Though I am not proud of my mistakes, I have learned from them. Who would I be today if I did not make my mistakes? This could only be a question that God could answer, and even then, I probably would not know.

I am more blessed today because I can see myself through the mistakes I have made. I have also learned from other people's mistakes because I take inventory of life. I do hope that this makes some sense to you. For I speak and think about blessings more on the way that God sees them for my life and not so much as the way I see them. For me, this is the courage that it takes for me to be blind in an unknown future.

22

The Courage to Be Blind

I dedicate this chapter to all those who are either blind or have some type of vision impairment.

Through my years of being blind, I have acknowledged the love for people, especially my family. My blindness has brought me to a place in my life that I have never been before! As I continue to accept my blindness something I cannot change, I am starting to understand what courage is and how powerful it can be to change the things that I can change.

You see, to me, courage and faith go hand in hand. You cannot experience one without the other and yet still succeed in dreams. Life is built around faith and courage. It takes both faith and courage to be able to comprehend what life is all about. Because it is just impossible to accomplish your goals without faith driving you forward and the courage to make it happen.

Through my blindness, I have learned so much about how to be courageous. For we who are blind learn to walk by faith and not by sight, and that is a proven fact. Just put on a black painted pair of goggles and go outside and cross the busy street by yourself and see if it really takes faith and courage. I am a living testimony of living by faith and courage, for I have done it. And I do believe that I could have not done it without the hand of God guiding me. Amen to that.

The most important part of my life is about having the courage to face the unknown world in this lifetime! You see, courage gives me the faith that I need to survive, facing the fear of the unknown. The unknown is that dark side of your soul that only the light can show you what is there. That is why it takes faith to step into the darkness and see what the light is showing you. There is a light at the end of that dark, cold, and scary tunnel. You must enter the darkness of that tunnel if you want to see what the light has in store for you at the end of the tunnel. It always gets the darkest before it reaches the dawn.

I have also come to acknowledge that it takes courage just to get out of bed each morning and face the new dawn ahead. And with boldness to endure any type of hardships that will come my way! In reality, it really takes courage just to wake up and be able to face the reality of life. Reality is life in itself! As for me, living in this rat race world being blind has become more challenging for me. I must face it each day with faith and courage, or I will not survive! I have faith in God and the courage to keep moving forward in life! God has given me strength and the wisdom to survive these dark and horrible days to come.

Faith and courage keep me on track with the reality of facing the unknown without fear. This is the only way that I can live my life to the fullest and still reach my dreams and my goals in this dark and painful world. No one can reach my dreams for me, for I must reach my own dreams by myself through faith, courage, and the grace of God's hand guiding me through this journey of life. No one can show me what to see if it is not there to look at.

Now for me to see what God has laid out for me in his plans, I must walk by faith and have courage to keep my head up when I am faced with the battles of life. God says that faith gives me the courage that I need to keep persevering through these battles. I also know that God gives me the endurance to face these challenges in life. You see, to me, faith is a way of the mind and the heart in knowing and believing in something that is not there and looking at it as though it is there. Faith will give you power to your thought process, because faith attracts God's attention. You see, when you attract God's attention, then everything and anything will be possible for you to do. For I know that there is nothing impossible for you to achieve whatever it is that you desire when God is on your side helping you in each and every step of the way. Just follow God, for he will lead you on that most perfect path every time.

God said, "As I walk through the shadow of the valley of death, I shall fear no evil," for I know my Lord is with me by my side because God walks with me where angels fear to tread (Psalm 23:4).

As I step out into this cold, dark, and evil world, I see what God is doing in the midst of my blindness. God is bringing me through these storms of life with peace in mind. God will set me high on his rock so that I can look over the horizon and see a new day dawning. For each day, I look forward to meeting God in the midst of all my pain and sorrows. For God holds my head up high to see what he has planned for me on each new given day.

My blindness has brought me to a new level of seeing the beauty that surrounds me. God's beauty is everywhere when I choose to look at it with my heart. Though blind, I can still see God's glory shining through these dark storm clouds. It is God who I put my trust in every day to help me persevere through these battles of life.

The challenges that life has brought me, I have endured them with perseverance. I refused to give up in times of discouraging moments, and I will continue fighting my way through these painful storms that life always seems to give. For each new painful level has brought me closer to God and His ways of living the life that He has set before me.

I now can live life to the fullest being blind. I now look at my blindness in a whole new level of a positive perspective, and I no longer allow my blindness to take control of me.

Reality is the best thing that I ever had to face in life, and though it has been painful to endure, I would not want my eyesight back because my blindness has brought me closer to God, and I now have more appreciation for the life that God gave me to live. I also believe that I can use my blindness as an opportunity to help others understand what life is all about.

You see, life is not about what you want or how you want it. Life is about what we can give and how we can give it. Since I have been blind, I have learned to give with a cheerful heart that God has created in me. Amen to that! To me, life has no limits, except for the only ones that you give to yourself. Take off your limits and allow God to work for you in your life.

Though reality may be painful to endure, with God's grace, you can face it with a positive attitude and persevere through the storms of life. Just remember that God is there in the midst of your pain and suffering, and He will walk you through to the other side. For every day, there is a new horizon through Christ! You can trust God to bring you peace in the midst of your storms. God promises that He will never leave you nor forsake you, and God will certainly *never* forget you.

And though life will still bring me some pain, I will still be able to accept my trials in life with a courageous heart that God gave me, and I will still move forward in life and be a blessing to others. My pain has given me the strength to grow and to live life in a godly way. God has prepared a way for me to live, and I will continue in His ways. I thank God for all that He has bestowed upon me, because He is the only one who can bring me through these storms and still give me a heart to *love*. This is the reason I can say, "I have peace-in the midst of pain and sufferings. "

I look at each new day as a picture that you paint. The beauty of each day allows me to see the dawn that arises each new given day and helps me to look for that new horizon, because just beyond that horizon is the glory of God in a new dawning day. Praise God for the life that He has given me to live. Thank you, Lord. They say that a picture is worth a thousand words, but God is worth more.

As I end my book with these final words, I would like to talk about the acknowledgement of my future destiny, in the hopes that I can reach out to other people and help them to understand life's greatest challenges and to understand that God uses our trials and our pain to live our life to its fullest.

You see, God blesses us through our pain even though we do not feel His presence. Our pain becomes too unbearable to feel His presence, and therefore we start to think that God does not care and that He does not love us. But whether you believe so or not, God does love us even more during the midst of our pain, because He feels the pain too.

There is certainly one thing I have noticed, and for the life of me, I had to really endure it. It is called attracting enemies. The more I draw closer to God during the midst of my pain and trials, the more enemies I seem to attract. Go figure. I know that Satan really hates it when I draw close to God, and therefore He tries even harder to see to it my pain becomes intolerable, just so I can focus on my pain and not focus on God. That is Satan's way of getting my attention. This is also Satan's strategy to get the best of me. But of course, this is His job, and this is what He does to everyone. Pain is His game, and Satan is out to see who is going to win. As long as I know His tricks, I can and will beat Him at His own game. And God promises to help me remain strong during the midst of my darkest hours. I just got to praise God for that.

It is my deepest appreciation to give God all of the glory for this book. God has given me the wisdom and the understanding that I needed to write this inspiring message, in the hopes of helping others. I ask God, as you read this book, to bless you and help you in your weakest and darkest moments of your journey in life. And thank you to all who read this book.

God bless you!

ABOUT THE AUTHOR

My name is Juanita R. Vedder, and I have three grown beautiful daughters who are very supportive with me about my blindness. I am also married to a very wonderful God-given man, who has been in my life for the past twenty-four years and has given me the best support I need for my blindness. My husband, Frank Vedder, and my three children (Jessica Calderon, married; Tabatha Groce, married, and Trisha Vedder)—I could not of ask for a better family than them. I praise God for the beautiful and supportive family that He has bestowed upon me. I was born with this eye disease called retinitis pigmentosa, a disease that deteriorates the retina. I have one older brother who has the same disease. The doctors say that there is no cure for this type of disease, and yes, it is hereditary. Though I have this eye disease, it is still my greatest desire to push life beyond its limits and to succeed in making my dreams a reality. For God Himself gave me the strength and the courage to live my life the way He has planned it for me. I shall live my life one day at a time, teaching others to follow the same God-given pattern. With God, all things are possible. Thank you, dear Lord, for I know that someday I will reach my final destiny with praise and thanksgiving in my heart.

www.ingramcontent.com/pod-product-compliance
Lightning Source LLC
Chambersburg PA
CBHW020318130626
46549CB00003B/918